1

For The Record

Man Passes Dozens Awaiting 20-Pointer

Adam Taylor of Cambridge, Ohio, noticed three bucks that stood out from their bachelor group in June 2002.

Taylor followed these bucks for three months, trying to decide which one to hunt. Two of the bucks made the decision for him when they suddenly left one day a month before bow-season.

The remaining buck looked to be a 13-pointer, and Taylor didn't think it looked overly big in his low-quality binoculars. Still, he decided to hunt it.

On Taylor's first bow-hunt of the season, he saw 14 bucks, but he didn't see the 13-pointer he'd watched the last few months.

The second evening was more of the same.

On the third evening, the big boy came right underneath Taylor's stand, but it was after shooting hours.

Each night Taylor moved closer to where he saw the buck come out the third night, hoping to catch it during shooting hours.

On Oct. 16, everything came together on his sixth hunt.

Taylor was late getting to his tree stand. About a half-hour after he got to his stand, Taylor saw the big buck running about 45 yards away. The buck turned and was walking out of sight when Taylor grunted.

The buck turned and approached, then stopped broadside about 35 yards away.

When Taylor drew, his arrow fell off his rest. There was nothing he could do, because he didn't want to spook the buck, so he held at full-draw for what seemed like forever.

When the buck finally looked away, Taylor grabbed the arrow with his teeth, flopped it onto the rest, and let it fly.

The arrow caught the buck in the spine and dropped it instantly. A quick follow-up shot finished the buck.

Fearing ground shrinkage, Taylor was afraid to look at his buck.

However, he couldn't believe it when he counted 20 points, including two drop tines. The trophy scored 183 3/8 nontypical, and Taylor was ecstatic.

Four months of watching the buck had paid off. With all the time Taylor spends scouting, it might be time for new binoculars.

JEFF AKERS shot this 182$^{2}/_{8}$-inch 10-pointer with his bow after arthritis forced him to crossbow-hunt for years. The buck was 6$^{1}/_{2}$ years old.

The Little Book of Big Bucks

FROM THE PUBLISHERS OF DEER & DEER HUNTING MAGAZINE

— 2003 Edition —

Published by
Krause Publications
700 E. State St. • Iola, WI 54990-0001
Telephone: 715/445-2214 fax: 715/445-4087
World Wide Web: www.deeranddeerhunting.com

Please call or write for our free catalog of outdoor publications.
Our toll-free number to place an order or obtain a free catalog is 800-258-0929.

Library of Congress Catalog Number: 2003106645

ISBN: 0-87349-723-6
Printed in the United States of America

Contents

The Little Book of Big Bucks is published by *Deer & Deer Hunting Magazine*, 700 E. State St., Iola, WI 54990-0001. To submit material for future editions, see our ad on Page 208.

Cover photo by Denver Bryan

Editor's Note

By Joe Shead

For the Love of Antlers

I'll never forget my first deer hunt. I was 9, and although I was too young to tote my own rifle, it was just as well. I was dripping with youthful excitement and squirming like a Mexican jumping bean. There was no way I could have held a gun steady.

My dad was equally nervous. It took five shots, but he dropped a half-rack 4-pointer, and from the moment I touched that buck's gray, bristle-like hairs, I enlisted as a life-long deer hunter.

There's a certain mystique about bucks and their antlers.

From short spikes to wide, heavy racks, antlers are just plain interesting — and unique.

You can't look at a set of antlers without pondering deeply. Why did the buck grow only half a rack? What caused this wide spot in this tine? Did this odd-racked buck sustain an injury to the opposite side of its body?

Although all antlers are fascinating, hunters have a special infatuation with large racks.

Growing a set of trophy antlers is no easy task. Bucks must avoid predators, human and otherwise, not to mention traffic and natural disasters. Plus, genetics, nutrition and other factors determine the size of a buck's antlers. Also, it may take several years to grow big antlers, and most bucks simply won't live long enough to grow large racks.

But some do.

This book is a compilation of success stories from hunters who, by luck or skill, killed bragging-sized bucks.

Chapter 1, "For The Record," details the hunts of a few hunters who killed record-class deer.

We've all heard stories about rookies who killed huge deer. Chapter 2 tells some of their stories.

Patience is a critical part of hunting. Chapter 3, "Worth The Wait," shows its reward.

Killing a big buck is truly memorable. "My Best Buck" is filled with stories of hunters who tagged their best deer.

Chapter 5, "A Family Affair," reveals how deer hunting binds families together.

"Antlers Across America," is a roundup of bucks killed across the country and in Canada.

Chapter 7, "Strange Places," proves that deer aren't restricted to living in woodlots and fields.

Lastly, Chapter 8, "Big Buck References," is filled with information to help you kill your buck of a lifetime.

Whether or not we ever kill record-class bucks, it is the thrill of the chase and the love of deer that keeps us in the woods, year after year. This book celebrates the success of those who have killed nice bucks, and the determination of those who wish to.

ADAM TAYLOR of Cambridge, Ohio, bagged this 20-point buck after watching it and two other impressive bucks for four months. The drop tine buck scored 183³/₈ nontypical.

Medicine Gives New Life To Illinois Bow-Hunter

The 2000 bow-season was a special one for Jeff Akers of West Point, Ill. After being diagnosed with a type of arthritis in his spine in 1995, he needed to hunt with a crossbow. While crossbow-hunting enabled him to spend more time in the woods each fall, it wasn't the same as hunting with a bow. However, in January 2000, his doctor gave him a new medicine that relieved his pain and allowed him to again hunt with a bow.

The 2000 hunt was extra sweet because Akers was confident a huge buck lurked his property. His brother found a set of sheds in Spring 1999 that would have netted about 170 inches. Akers saw the buck once while crossbow hunting, but couldn't get a shot. As far as he knew, the buck was still alive, but no one had seen it for nearly a year.

On opening day of Illinois' 2000 archery season, Akers was equipped with his new bow — one with a lighter draw weight that wouldn't aggravate his spine. He was anxious to experience the feeling of shooting a deer with a compound bow again, and when a mature doe passed by him at 20 yards that morning, he shot it.

Shooting the doe built his confidence. He now knew he had the strength to shoot a buck.

On Nov. 10, Akers hunted the stand where he'd seen the huge 10-pointer the year before. Early that morning, Akers heard a pair of turkeys heading his way. He had a turkey tag and decided he'd shoot. Just then he heard rustling in the leaves and saw an 8-pointer 25 yards away. Akers drew and grunted with his mouth. The buck stopped, and Akers sent the arrow. The buck went 70 yards before expiring.

Akers was excited with his first bow-killed buck in years, but the best was yet to come.

The next morning he hunted from the same stand. As daylight broke, Akers saw a good buck. He picked up his rattling antlers and tickled them together and grunted a few times. This seemed to get the buck's attention, but the buck seemed focused behind Akers. Just then, Akers heard thrashing behind him.

Less than 70 yards away, Akers saw the big 10-pointer raking its antlers on a cedar tree. Akers gave a snort-wheeze, and the big buck came in sidestepping and grunting with its ears pinned back. When the buck's head disappeared behind a tree, Akers grunted and the buck stopped 15 yards away. Akers steadied his sight pin the best he could and shot. The buck leaped twice and stopped. At first Akers thought he'd missed, but then he saw the deer bleeding. The buck wobbled and fell within sight.

The $6\frac{1}{2}$-year-old 10-pointer netted $182\frac{2}{8}$ typical inches.

Akers' life has improved 100 percent since taking the new medicine. Shooting the buck was the icing on the cake.

SAM COLLORA shot this massive 13-point buck in Iowa. He'd first seen the big-footed buck when it was an 8-pointer the previous year.

Disappearing Buck Reappears Just in Time

In 2000, Sam Collora saw a huge 8-pointer. Even though the buck had only eight points, Collora knew it was large enough to make the Boone and Crockett record book.

However, he didn't get a chance to find out. The buck "disappeared" throughout fall and winter. Collora didn't see the buck the following summer, but he did notice some large, deep hoof prints. Although there was no way to know it was the same deer, Collora knew a heavy deer frequented his area.

By January, Collora's archery and muzzleloader buck tags remained unfilled. He was holding out for a big buck, and it looked like it wasn't going to be Collora's year.

On Jan. 7, 2002 Collora took to the woods. A doe came in close, and Collora had his finger on the trigger, but decided not to shoot.

The following evening, Collora set up in a wild plum thicket on a point that projects into a field.

That evening another doe appeared, and Collora prepared for a shot. However, when the doe looked behind her, he decided to wait to see what was following her.

Moments later a huge buck emerged and ran to the doe.

As soon as Collora saw the buck, he reverted his attention back to the doe. He hoped the buck would follow the doe, but Collora knew if he spooked the doe, his chances at the buck were over, and his muzzleloader was still on his lap. He couldn't afford to make any movements that would spook the doe.

The doe ran to the edge of the field, then turned and stopped 60 yards from Collora. It walked to Collora's left, then walked over the crest of the hill and disappeared.

With the doe out of sight, Collora raised his muzzleloader to shooting position, then turned his attention toward the buck. He hoped it would follow the doe, and within moments it did.

The buck ran from at a "fast trot." Collora aimed in front of the deer, swung and pulled the trigger.

The buck continued in the line it was running and it, too, crested the hill and disappeared. Collora popped up from his position on the ground and tried to watch the fleeing buck and reload at the same time, which was more than he could handle in his excitement. However, Collora didn't need a second shot. The buck fell at the bottom of the hill.

From his position, Collora couldn't see the deer's body, but could see one-third of the rack. That's when he realized how huge the buck really was. He let out a "war hoop you could hear for three counties."

It wasn't until he reached the downed deer that Collora realized the 13-pointer was the same buck he'd seen before when it was an 8-pointer. And one look at the buck's snowshoe-like feet confirmed this was the deer that had made the large, deep tracks.

The 13-pointer grossed 204 inches and featured four tines measuring more than 12 inches.

Collora, who owns Mrs. Doe Pee's Buck Lures, said he felt overwhelmingly privileged to shoot the buck.

FOLLOWING HIS 4½-year-old son's advice, Shane Landrum bagged this 150-class 11-pointer.

Toddler Picks Setup, Father Tags Trophy

On Oct. 16, 2002, Shane Landrum of Kirkersville, Ohio, was running late. He hurried to get ready for his evening bow-hunt, and his inquisitive 4½-year-old son, Triston's, endless questions weren't helping Landrum get to his stand any faster.

Landrum had been meaning to take Triston hunting for a while and decided to take him along that evening.

Landrum remembered he'd left his bow at his parking area earlier that morning, and asked Triston if he should get the bow or go without it and simply watch deer for the evening. Triston (who Landrum claims has seen every deer hunting video ever made) emphatically told his father to retrieve his bow!

Bow in hand, the pair headed into the woods. Given the choice between an elevated stand or a ground blind, the adventurous toddler selected the elevated stand, and after a painstakingly careful climb, and some clever rigging of a safety harness, father and son made it into the stand.

Within minutes, six does entered a soybean field and began eating. Landrum was thrilled that his son finally had a chance to see wild deer up close, and at that point the hunt was already an overwhelming success. But it was about to get even better.

Fifteen minutes later, Landrum thought he heard a deer grunt. After a few minutes, he thought he only imagined it, but then he saw a huge buck entering the field about 125 yards away. The buck was chasing does and scent-checking across the soybean field.

Landrum didn't even react to the buck, thinking a shot was out of the question, but the buck seemed to have interest in one particular doe, and soon the doe was only 20 yards from the elevated hunters and the buck was coming!

It was then that Landrum suddenly realized he was going to get a shot at the buck. Up until that point, he hadn't even imagined it would come close enough to shoot.

The buck approached very cautiously, and was headed for a shooting lane downwind of the father and son duo. However, the buck paid more attention to the doe than the wind, and when the buck entered the shooting lane, Landrum shot.

Triston did an amazing job of staying quiet, and probably was more calm than his excited father.

Landrum has now shot three Pope-and-Young-class bucks in the last five years, and each year he asks himself if hunting can get any better. Now he really doubts it. Shooting the 150-class 11-pointer in front of his son was a moment Landrum won't soon forget!

MICHELE TURNER of Mershon, Ga., shot this 8-pointer in Pierce County. It is the largest buck ever shot in the county.

Georgia Woman Shoots County's Biggest Buck

Michele Turner of Mershon, Ga., has hunted every year since deer season opened in Pierce County in 1980. The veteran whitetail hunter now finds herself in the record book after killing the county's largest buck ever.

In November 2002, Turner and her husband, Wayne were hunting from their homemade steel platform stands located along food plots on their 50-acre farm. They are blessed to live in good deer country. The area is highly agricultural, and the neighbors practice good deer management. The Turner farm is also bordered on three sides by woods, and a brushy creek borders the west end, providing deer with plenty of high-quality cover.

Before sunrise, Turner heard deer milling around in the brush near her stand. She hoped the deer wouldn't leave the area before she had enough light to see them.

Soon she heard a deer walking very close by — she knew it had to be within 20 yards. Turner heard the frozen grass crunching under the deer's hoofs as it walked.

It was now light enough to see, and Turner waited for the deer to step into a mowed strip.

Suddenly she saw a doe run out into the food plot and stop about 100 yards away. Turner pulled back the hammer on her .30-30, put the scope's cross hairs behind the doe's shoulder, and pulled the trigger. The doe collapsed.

As Turner worked the lever, a larger deer appeared right behind the fallen doe. Turner instantly saw the buck's large rack, and although Wayne had taught her to ignore antlers when shooting, she couldn't help but gawk at the rack.

The buck was moving fast, so Turner whistled and the buck stopped 125 yards away.

Turner touched off the shot and the buck stumbled as it fled. Her shots were only three seconds apart!

Turner whistled for her husband and yelled uncharacteristically. It was then that he knew she'd shot a big buck, and he cut straight through thick, head-high briars to reach her.

The Turners got their trailing dog, but the buck had only gone 50 yards before falling and was easy to find.

Turner's record-setting 8-pointer weighed 180 pounds and the 16 1/8-inch-wide rack netted 139 1/8 inches.

The Turners brought the deer into town to show some friends, and so many people stopped to see the deer, someone actually called the police, thinking there was an accident.

Turner said she hasn't had her picture taken so many times since her wedding day, and now people in adjoining towns recognize her because they've seen her picture with her big buck everywhere!

JOHN MILLER of Hartville, Ohio, shot this 14-point buck Nov. 7, 2001, with his crossbow after missing the chance to draw his bow on the deer eight days earlier. The rack measured 201⅝ nontypical inches, and the 14-pointer had an estimated live weight of 285 pounds.

Injured Crossbow Hunter Gets Second Chance

On Oct. 30, 2001, John Miller of Hartville, Ohio, experienced something most deer hunters dream of: A huge 14-point buck walked within 20 yards of him while he was bowhunting.

But he didn't shoot.

In March of 2001, Miller broke his wrist, and planned on hunting the entire bow-season with a crossbow instead of with his compound bow. However, a week before bow season, Miller discovered that enough strength had returned to his arm that he could shoot his bow again, so he brushed up on his shooting and toted the compound afield.

Miller could have killed the 14-pointer with his bow, but it slipped in on him, before he had a chance to draw. Miller would have had a clear shot, and the buck stood still 25 yards away for a minute or so, but Miller couldn't risk moving to pull back his bow.

However, he nearly got a shot at the deer. When the buck was 30 yards away, Miller started to draw his bow, but the buck turned and looked in his direction, and Miller stopped and held at mid-draw.

When the buck finally moved on a minute or two later, Miller didn't have enough strength to pull back his bow again.

However, Miller was confident he hadn't spooked the buck and continued to hunt in the same area the next few days. However, he brought his crossbow instead of his bow to make sure he wouldn't have trouble shooting if the big boy appeared again.

Miller's hunting area was alive with deer during early November, and he passed up six bucks during the first week of the month, hoping the big 14-pointer would return. It did.

At 5:15 p.m. Nov. 7, eight nights after Miller had first seen the giant buck, Miller saw it again. The 14-pointer entered a soybean field about 150 yards from Miller's stand. The buck was chasing a doe. After about 15 minutes, the deer had closed the distance to Miller's stand to about 60 yards, and things were looking promising.

Miller grunted a few times, and a yearling doe appeared in the woods 25 yards behind him. The doe caught the buck's attention, and the buck ambled in the doe's direction.

However, when the big buck reached the doe-in-estrous scent trail Miller had laid down with his boots, it forgot about the doe and followed the trail right to Miller's stand.

This time Miller didn't have to worry about his weakened wrist, and when the buck stood 15 yards away, Miller touched the trigger on his crossbow.

At the shot the buck acted hit, and Miller was confident he'd hit the deer, but he wasn't sure where. The buck ran 40 yards and stopped, and after standing for about a minute, collapsed.

Miller's 14-point buck was a real bruiser. Its rack measured 201 5/8 nontypical inches and Miller's taxidermist estimated the buck's live weight was 285 pounds.

JIM FAVREAU traveled to Illinois to shoot this 16-point nontypical. The buck grossed 188⅝ inches.

Maine Hunter Finds His Trophy in Illinois

Jim Favreau of Pittston, Maine, owns an archery shop, and is crazy about bow-hunting. To fuel his passion, he makes an annual trek to Illinois to hunt big bucks.

In 2001, he and four friends hunted two Illinois properties. The group focused mostly on the larger parcel the first week of the hunt, as wind direction was generally in the south. However, when Nov. 8, rolled in on a north wind, Favreau headed to a stand he'd placed on the smaller property.

Favreau's stand abutted a large tract of timber. Several trails crisscrossed the area, and Favreau hoped his buck decoy would draw passing bucks in close enough for a shot.

Favreau saw three small bucks, a doe and a buck fawn. Then, at about 5 p.m., he heard movement and saw a large antler moving in the woods.

Soon, Favreau saw a doe and a mature buck in the woods. Favreau bleated and the buck stopped and looked in his direction, but continued on. Favreau tried a bleat call with a grunt call. The buck stopped again, scraped the ground with its hoof, and kept walking.

Minutes passed with the deer still in the woods. Finally, the doe stepped into the field, with the buck in tow. However, instead of staying with the doe, the buck walked toward Favreau, apparently to inspect the grunts and bleats.

Favreau drew and the buck stopped at 29 yards, but only offered a straight-on spine shot. Favreau passed in hopes of a better shot. At 25 yards the buck stopped and raced back to the doe.

Favreau's hopes sank. The deer were now 65 yards away, and Favreau's only hope was that the doe would investigate the deer decoy, but he didn't think it had even seen it.

When the doe got downwind of the decoy, it smelled the air and approached the fake, with the big buck right behind. The big nontypical circled between the decoy and Favreau and was only 20 yards away, but Favreau couldn't shoot.

The buck tried to corral the doe, but it bolted, and the buck gave chase.

The buck was now 40 yards away. Favreau, a 3-D tournament shooter who practices out to 50 yards, bleated with his mouth, and when the buck stopped, he launched his arrow.

The buck ran toward Favreau and stopped at 20 yards, and Favreau sent a second arrow. However, his first shot was good, and the buck collapsed after the second lethal shot.

Favreau was surprised by the buck's rack. At first he thought it was only a good-sized 8-pointer, but when he recovered the deer, he saw his big nontypical sported 16 points and grossed 188 5/8 inches. The deer field dressed at 210 pounds.

BILL HART killed this 178⅝-inch Indiana 12-pointer Oct. 28, 2001. It was the largest buck killed in Indiana during the 2001-2002 season.

Management Helps Man Shoot Buck of a Lifetime

Noble County, Ind., has long been regarded as one of the state's premier bow-hunting counties. The land is comprised of woodlots, thickets, rolling hills, creek bottoms, marshes and thick swamps interspersed with farm fields.

This combination of cover and feed helps Noble County produce a crop of trophy bucks, as Bill Hart, of Kendallville, found out. But one other thing contributed to his successful 2001 bow-season.

In 1996, Hart took a deer hunting trip to Michigan. On the property he hunted, bucks with fewer than eight points or a spread less than the width of the ears were protected.

Hart pondered the thought of trying this idea in his hunting area.

Hart, his brother and some friends instituted a similar program on their 150 acres of farmland in 1997.

The group had always used deer drives in the past, and after shooting only one deer the first year of the program, some hunters weren't too fond of the idea.

However, over the next few seasons, the hunters noticed an increase in the number of larger-racked bucks they saw.

In 2001, the group's management program paid off in a big way.

Oct. 28 was clear, cool and calm — perfect for deer movement.

Hart reached his stand about 2:45 p.m. By 3 p.m., he had his bow and video camera ready for action. He didn't have to wait long.

After a few minutes had passed, Hart bleated twice, and a monster buck responded immediately.

The buck was heading in the wrong direction, but turned to the right and proceeded down a four-wheeler path and into a shooting lane about 30 yards away.

Hart recalls seeing the arrow hit the buck and fall to the ground on the opposite side as if in slow motion. Hart waited about 45 minutes after the shot before climbing down from his stand.

He checked to see that he had made a good hit, then went for help. After tracking the buck for about 100 yards, Hart and his companions found the monster 12-pointer.

Hart's buck was the highest-scoring typical buck killed in Indiana during the 2001-2002 season. The 12-pointer field dressed at 240 pounds and scored 178 5/8, placing it seventh in the Hoosier State's all-time record book.

And after slow initial acceptance of the quality-management program, Hart's group believes in it, and Hart's companions are intent on shooting an even bigger deer!

— Dean Weimer

SHERRY BRENDLE of Louisville, Ohio, shot this 11-point buck from her husband's deer stand while he was napping.

2

Beginner's Luck

Woman Shoots Buck While Husband Naps

Opening day of Ohio's 2001 gun season dawned extremely foggy.

Sherry Brendle of Louisville, Ohio, was hunting in the place where she'd shot her first deer two years earlier, and her husband, Karl, hunted nearby.

The fog ebbed and flowed, and Brendle only saw a few does, due to limited visibility. Brendle decided to check in with her husband to see if he'd had better luck.

Karl had seen a pair of bucks but couldn't shoot because he used his buck tag during the archery season. Sherry decided Karl's spot was better, so she stayed with her husband, who kicked back for a nap while she watched for deer.

Brendle's neck was sore for days after craning to see in all directions. But it paid off when she spied three does and a mature buck.

Brendle tapped her husband on the leg and reported what she saw. He told her to crank up the power on her scope.

She thought the buck was just an average 7- or 8-pointer, but when the does started running and the buck ran after them, she decided the buck was big enough to shoot.

She shouldered her .54-caliber muzzleloader. It was so heavy the barrel was moving in circles, but she pulled the trigger, and through the smoke, she saw the buck lying on the ground. Brendle reloaded just in case she needed a second shot, but she was so excited and was shaking so wildly that only half the powder went down the muzzle!

Karl had already started making his way to the buck, and Sherry ran after him, losing her boot on the way!

Karl quickly counted 10 points and exclaimed "You got the big one!"

Sherry counted the tines three times and corrected her husband. The buck was actually an 11-pointer.

Karl said he'll never have a chance to shoot a buck bigger than his wife's 11-pointer, but she isn't so sure. She thinks sometimes all you need is a little bit of luck!

Of course, it's a lot easier to shoot a big buck if you stay awake on your deer stand!

Moving Decision Leads to Big Buck

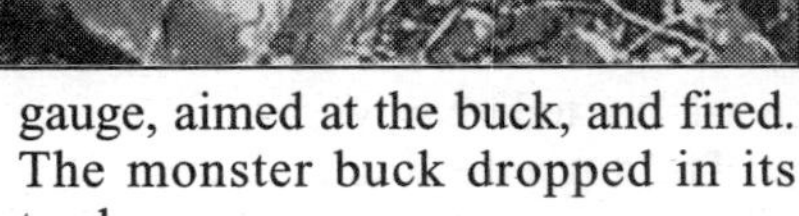

At his young age, it's hard to say if T.J. Rosenberg of Hanoverton, Ohio, is an incredible woodsman or just plain lucky.

Either way, it doesn't matter. On Nov. 26, 2001, the young hunter killed the kind of buck most hunters can only dream about.

HUNTER: **T.J. Rosenberg**
DATE: **Nov. 26, 2001**
LOCATION: **Columbiana Co., Ohio**
METHOD: **Gun**
RACK: **17-point buck, 175-class**

It was opening day of Ohio's 2001 gun-season. Rosenberg and his father left their house in Columbiana County at about 6 a.m. on a cold, clear November morning. They climbed into their deer stands around 6:30 a.m.

The Rosenbergs sat for about $2\frac{1}{2}$ hours, but by 9 a.m., T.J. decided it was time to move. His father agreed, so they moved to a new area.

Rosenberg had only been sitting in his new spot for about 20 minutes when he heard leaves crunching behind him. Rosenberg spotted a doe, and right behind it was a huge buck.

The deer were staring at him from only about 25 yards away. Rosenberg sat stock still. When the doe looked away, Rosenberg quickly shouldered his youth-model 20 gauge, aimed at the buck, and fired. The monster buck dropped in its tracks.

Rosenberg's father, who was positioned about 40 yards away, heard the doe run away, and assumed that's what his son was shooting at.

T.J. put his arms over his head, indicating antlers, and yelled that the buck was down. Rosenberg's father cautiously came over to investigate.

When he looked up the hill and saw the monster whitetail on the ground, he couldn't believe what he saw.

The 17-point buck's rack grossed $175\frac{3}{8}$ Boone and Crockett inches after the required 60-day drying period.

Father and son were elated over T.J.'s big buck. That night, the Rosenbergs' doorbell rang nonstop as guests came over to see the young man's monstrous 17-point buck.

Maryland Girl Cashes in on Buck Parade

LAURA KREIS shot a 12-pointer and and a 10-pointer within minutes of each other while hunting in Maryland.

Lightning struck twice within 15 minutes for Laura Kreis during Maryland's 2001 gun season.

Kreis had been sitting on her stand for a couple hours on the second Saturday of gun season when a doe trotted straight toward her. The 16-year-old Kreis shot a doe during the state's youth hunt and another on opening day of the regular season and had decided to hold out for bucks with her two remaining tags.

Seconds later, Kreis noticed a nontypical rack bobbing through a thicket and realized a buck was heading for an opening 30 yards from her stand. Kreis' heart raced as she put her scope's cross-hairs on the opening, while keeping track of the 12-pointer's movements with her other eye. The doe passed through the opening, but the buck paused. Kreis stayed ready, and moments later, her patience paid off when the buck presented her the shot she'd been waiting for. The buck bolted into the thicket at the shot.

Kreis radioed her father, Dan, who told her to sit tight, as it was still fairly early. Reluctantly, Kreis followed her father's orders, but the question of whether she'd hit the deer tormented her. The decision to wait didn't seem so bad when a 4-pointer ran by minutes later. Kreis again held off, not wanting to end the season so soon. But another 10 minutes was all the longer her season would last, as a 10-pointer was trailing the doe that had passed earlier. It, too, stopped in the opening, and Kreis fired. After the shot's echo faded, Kreis again radioed her father, who couldn't believe her amazing story. But even before her father reached her, a 3-pointer trotted by Kreis' hot spot.

Kreis, along with her father, cousins and uncles, found the two bucks within a few yards of each other. The 12-pointer scored 160 typical and 175 $^{4}/_{8}$ nontypical on the Boone & Crockett scale.

Michigan Hunter Gets Late-Season Surprise

By early November, the 2000 deer season was looking dismal for Adam Nieman. It was the first year Nieman passed up young bucks in hopes of bagging a mature whitetail, and though he'd seen Pope-and-Young-class bucks on his neighbor's property where he hunted, he never got a chance at them.

Nieman's neighbors hunt the property during Michigan's gun season, so Nieman had to go elsewhere with his rifle.

HUNTER: **Adam Nieman**
DATE: **Dec. 11, 2000**
LOCATION: **Michigan**
METHOD: **Muzzleloader**
RACK: **12-point buck**

The first two days of gun season, Nieman hunted public land with his brothers, but saw only does. Frustrated, he knew he had to find a better place to hunt.

Nieman told his girlfriend about his frustration, and she suggested he hunt on the 20 acres behind her house. Only 8 acres were wooded and the rest of the property was overgrown agricultural fields. However, it had received no hunting pressure, but the surrounding woods were hunted heavily. Nieman decided that it was worth a shot.

On Nov. 17, Nieman made a low-pressure still-hunt to scout the property. He was excited by what he saw. There was plenty of thick undergrowth for deer to bed in, and there were numerous fresh scrapes and rubs. Nieman found a where the field went into the woods. An old stump made a perfect natural blind, and he would be downwind of any deer entering the field. He returned two days later.

On his first hunt from the stump blind, Nieman shot a small 8-pointer. He was excited that he found success in his new hunting spot, but he still wanted to tag a mature buck. He planned to hunt the muzzleloader season, but the task of shooting a buck was daunting because legally his second buck had to have at least four points on one side.

On Dec. 11, Nieman returned to the stump blind. Snow fell softly as evening approached, and Nieman drifted off to sleep for a moment. He had been watching seven does, and it was almost quitting time. He took one last look at the does, then spotted a big buck at the edge of the woods.

As Nieman raised the muzzleloader, the buck headed for the does. Nieman pushed the safety, and the click sounded like a .22 going off. The buck stopped and snapped its head in Nieman's direction, but was more interested in the does. The buck took two steps toward the does and stopped broadside 90 yards from Nieman in his stump blind. Nieman centered the 4X scope on the buck and squeezed the trigger. The flash of fire and billow of smoke hung in the air like fog.

Nieman's hands shook as he tried to reload the muzzleloader. He rushed to where the buck had stood, but found no blood or hair. He felt sick. He couldn't believe he missed.

Nieman started walking the runways that entered the clearing, looking for any sign of a wounded deer. He was about to leave for the night and return in the morning when he found a pin-drop of blood in the snow next to large, running deer tracks. Nieman followed the tracks and found the dead buck 70 yards from where he'd shot him.

It was a magnificent moment for Nieman, seeing his fallen trophy as the snow fluttered down.

Nieman's girlfriend had to help him load the buck into his truck, and his parents were amazed at the big-bodied 12-pointer.

Despite his good fortune, Nieman will have to find another spot to hunt because he broke up with his girlfriend. His friends still give him a hard time about that.

Buck Escapes Father, Harvested By Son

The hunt Coty Gall of York, Pa., experienced Nov. 2, 2002 will always be memorable for him. Unfortunately, it was one his father might hope to forget.

Coty and his father, Frank, were bow-hunting in Huntingdon County, Pa., that morning when a 6-point buck approached the elder Gall.

He'll never know if buck fever got the best of him or what happened, but somehow Frank missed the buck.

But the 6-pointer wasn't so lucky when it passed Coty's stand less than 5 minutes later.

Coty made the 30-yard shot, and the buck only traveled 40 yards before expiring.

This was Coty's sixth deer, and his largest.

Frank reports Coty hasn't ribbed him much about his miss, but he figures it's coming.

HUNTER:	**Coty Gall**
DATE:	**Nov. 2, 2002**
LOCATION:	**Huntingdon Co., Pennsylvania**
METHOD:	**Bow**
RACK:	**6-point buck**

New York Bow-Hunter Learns As He Goes

You have to forgive New York bow-hunter Rick Berg.

Berg is new to bow-hunting. In his first year of bow season on his very first hunt, he shot a doe. It must have seemed so very easy for him.

However, in 2001 he got an introduction to a more typical bow-hunting lifestyle — with a sweet ending.

It was the third to last day of bow-season, and Berg had yet to shoot a deer. However, he remained patient and didn't let his early success from his inaugural season overshadow his hunt.

HUNTER: **Rick Berg**
DATE: **Nov. 16, 2001**
LOCATION: **Geneseo, New York**
METHOD: **Bow**
RACK: **8-point buck, 120-class**

Berg's patience paid off when a wide-racked 8-pointer emerged from dense brush. Berg scrambled to lift his bow into shooting position and waited for the 8-pointer to wander into shooting range.

When the buck was 18 yards away, Berg released his arrow. At the shot, the buck lurched and the arrow hit the deer in the spine. The buck dropped and tried to regain its feet, but Berg sent another arrow to dispatch the buck.

Berg's wife is just as new to deer hunting as Berg is. She gave strict orders that he was to ensure that the deer didn't get blood in the van or on the driveway or even the lawn!

Berg wrapped his buck in a tarp, but blood still spilled on the driveway. He wanted a picture of his trophy to remember the hunt, but he hadn't brought a camera for an in-the-field picture.

His wife agreed to take a picture of Berg and his buck in their lawn, but he couldn't get blood on the grass. Berg thought if he propped the buck up, using the front legs to hold the belly off the ground, he might be able to keep blood from spilling out of the field-dressed 8-pointer. It worked!

You can't argue with success and a little ingenuity, but when Berg showed his friends a picture of his deer, they all laughed. One person suggested the picture was Berg posing with the neighbor's dog with a set of antlers. Another said that Berg was posing with a live deer!

Despite the ribbing, Berg is becoming a proficient bow-hunter. The 8-pointer he bagged in only his second season grossed 120 inches and dressed at about 190 pounds.

Though the picture may look a little strange to veteran hunters, it's hard to argue with success!

Pat Reeve
Kansas, 2002
150-class 8-pointer

Hunter's First Buck Is One to Remember

Susan Dillman of Gettysburg, Pa., took up deer hunting eight years ago so she could spend more time outdoors with her husband, Jim. Today, Jim and Susan bowhunt and rifle-hunt, and Jim had killed a few does and a spike buck, but by the 2002 hunting season, Susan had never even shot at a deer. However, with a little luck and a prayer, her luck changed during the 2002 Pennsylvania rifle season.

HUNTER: **Susan Dillman**
DATE: **Opening Day 2002**
LOCATION: **Pennsylvania**
METHOD: **.308 Rifle**
RACK: **11-point buck**

On opening morning, Susan and Jim hunted public land, but they didn't see a deer. They returned home to rest before heading out for their afternoon hunt. Susan's father stopped by and asked if they wanted to join him on a friend's private property. The pair jumped at the chance.

Susan's dad showed them the lay of the land, and Susan chose a homemade tree stand near the corner of a woods and a soybean field.

Susan entered the stand at about 1:30. About 45 minutes later she heard tree branches rattling. She knew it had to be a buck, but she didn't know it would be the biggest buck she'd ever seen!

Fifteen minutes later, an 11-point buck stepped into view. Susan's heart hammered. Susan had never even aimed at a deer, much less a buck. She collected herself, and when she had the cross hairs on its vitals, she squeezed the trigger on her .308.

The buck reared up like Susan had seen on hunting shows and darted into thick cover. Susan waited 30 minutes before trailing the deer.

When she found no sign of the deer, her bliss turned to depression. Jim and her father joined the search, but they found nothing and decided to look again in the morning.

The following morning, after an uneventful hunt, Susan's father suggested they look for the 11-pointer again.

Susan and her father walked into the thick cover along a stream. Susan's gaze fell on a tree, and her heart jumped. There, under the tree, was her deer! Her father ran over and gave her a hug and a kiss, and they radioed Jim.

Susan decided patience and persistence pays off — especially when the first deer you shoot is also the largest buck you've ever seen!

Sore Throat Can't Keep Teen From Buck

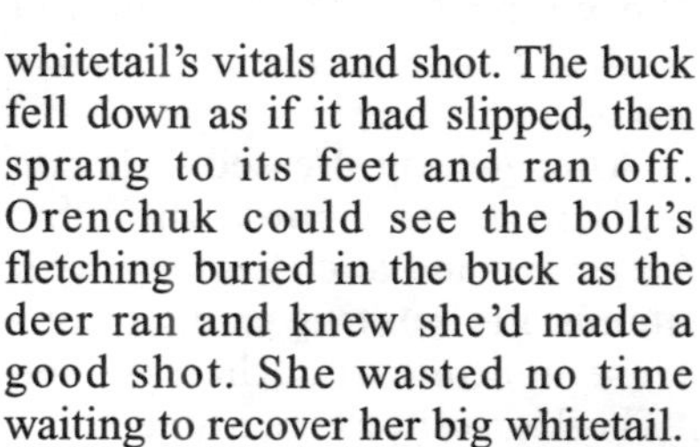

HUNTER: **Kristin Orenchuk**
DATE: **Oct. 28, 2001**
LOCATION: **Ohio**
METHOD: **Crossbow**
RACK: **13-point buck, 140-class**

Sometimes parents really do know what's best for their children.

Kristin Orenchuk of Paris, Ohio, learned that lesson during Ohio's 2001 deer season.

Orenchuk awoke on Oct. 28 with a sore throat and didn't want to go deer hunting. However, her father insisted she should go. Orenchuk followed her father's advice. Despite the sore throat, she got dressed, collected her gear and was sitting in her ground blind by 6 a.m.

Before she settled into her stand, Orenchuk put out some estrous scent. While she waited on that cloudy, 35-degree morning, she rattled and grunted occasionally while on stand, but a couple hours into the hunt, Orenchuk was still waiting for a buck to show.

Then, at 8:30, her luck changed. Orenchuk heard leaves crunching nearby, and moments later, a 13-point buck trotted into view. The buck trotted very close to Orenchuk's ground blind, then stopped to eat 15 yards in front of her.

Orenchuk shouldered her crossbow, aligned the sights on the big whitetail's vitals and shot. The buck fell down as if it had slipped, then sprang to its feet and ran off. Orenchuk could see the bolt's fletching buried in the buck as the deer ran and knew she'd made a good shot. She wasted no time waiting to recover her big whitetail.

Orenchuk went to get her father, and when they returned to where the buck had stood a few minutes later, they found a good blood trail and half of the bolt. Just as Orenchuk picked up the broken bolt, the buck jumped up and ran crashing into the woods, then there was silence.

The Orenchuks waited a few minutes, then continued trailing the deer. They found the wide-racked buck piled up about 100 yards away.

When they discovered the whitetail, the buck's rack was sticking up, and Orenchuk said the sight was truly awesome.

The 140-class 13-pointer had a field-dressed weight of 180 pounds.

What Are Friends For? Successful Deer Hunts!

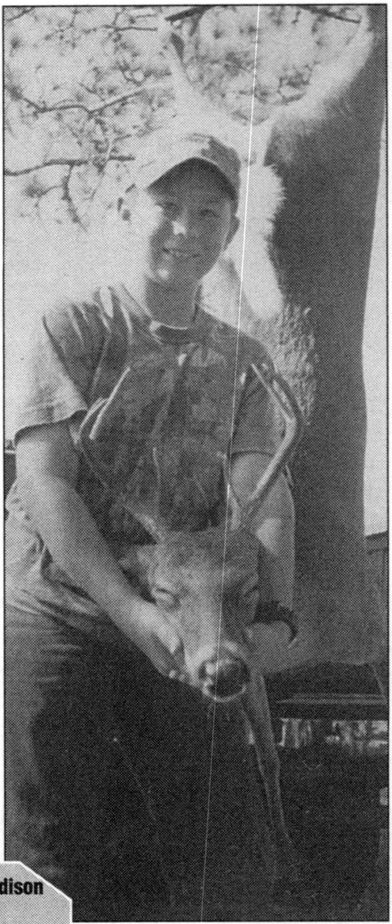

Eleven-year-old Thomas Addison of Hains City, Fla., owes part of his successful season to his friend, Jason Bowen.

Addison arrived in deer camp on a Friday night for opening weekend of Florida's deer season and stayed up until about 10 p.m. The next morning, he groggily awoke, and sat awake in bed for a half-hour before deciding he was too tired to go hunting.

However, Bowen wouldn't let the young hunter sleep in and rousted him from his warm, cozy bed.

After getting dressed, Addison walked to the cook shed for breakfast, and after learning what stands his hunting companions were hunting from, he selected "The Horseshoe" — a tree stand just east of hunting camp.

About 5 minutes after he climbed into his stand, four does appeared. Twenty minutes later, an 8-point buck arrived with its nose to the ground. It chased the does away, and Addison yelled, stopping the buck.

HUNTER: **Thomas Addison**
DATE: **2002**
LOCATION: **Pointciana, Florida**
METHOD: **.308 Rifle**
RACK: **8-point buck**

However, the buck stopped behind a palm tree and was practically right under Addison's stand. Luckily, after a few moments, the deer moved forward a few feet, and Addison raised his .308 and shot. The 8-point buck dropped in its tracks.

Addison excitedly climbed down from his stand, raced to his four-wheeler and sped back to camp.

When he burst through the door, Bowen asked why he was back so soon, and Addison blurted out that he'd shot a deer. Bowen raced him back to the four-wheeler and they returned to Addison's buck. The 8-pointer was so heavy it was all they could do to load it onto the four-wheeler.

Hunter Tags First Buck With Aid of Beagles

Daniel Singleton of Chesterfield, Va., had never shot a buck in six years of hunting. He'd shot a few does, but the bucks eluded him.

On Nov. 30, 2002, Singleton, his brother Tony and his uncle Teddy traveled to their hunt club. On the way, Singleton was given a good ribbing for missing several deer.

On the hunt club, dog handlers use beagles to push deer to posted hunters. On the morning of Singleton's hunt, the club decided to drive the "Big Woods," a hardwood forest bordered by pines with a creek running through the middle.

HUNTER: **Daniel Singleton**
DATE: **Nov. 30, 2002**
LOCATION: **Virginia**
METHOD: **Shotgun**
RACK: **10-point buck**

Singleton was positioned beside the creek in a hardwood bottom. The area is a frequent escape route of pressured deer.

The drive began at 7:30 a.m. After a few minutes of relative silence, the dogs opened up. They had caught the trail of a big 10-pointer, and they were heading toward Singleton! The commotion was so loud Singleton said it sounded like five deer were running through the woods

The buck was sneaking through some small pines 35 yards from Singleton when it spotted the young hunter. Singleton already had his shotgun shouldered and aimed at the buck when it stopped. He fired and the buck fell, but he needed two more shots to kill the deer quickly.

Singleton's uncle radioed him to find out if he'd gotten a deer. Singleton answered that he'd shot a nice buck. His uncle rushed over to see.

Singleton was in disbelief, and pretty excited, the rest of the morning. Later, when his father radioed him to see what was happening, Singleton told him about the 10-pointer.

"Does it have any size to it?" his father asked.

"Yeah, a little bit," Singleton joked.

The buck had a 17-inch spread.

Tracy Drury
Iowa, 2001
140-class 8-pointer

Mark Drury

Inexperienced Hunter Makes Up for Lost Time

Gary Fitzke of Louisburg, Kan., had never hunted, but his stepdad, Charles Putnam, has hunted for more than 50 years in Georgia. Fitzke listened intently to Putnam's hunting stories, and decided to take up the sport. With Putnam as a mentor, they planned a hunt for Fall 2001.

The first day of his hunt, Fitzke shot a doe, and the next day he bagged a small 7-pointer. He was hooked.

On the first morning of the 2002 hunt, Fitzke was excited. However, for a while he grew concerned after he struggled to find his stand in the dark.

He saw three does in the morning, and hoped a buck would follow, but none did.

HUNTER: **Gary Fitzke**
DATE: **Opening Day 2002**
LOCATION: **Kansas**
METHOD: **Rifle**
RACK: **10-point buck**

At 11 a.m., he rendezvoused with Putnam, who ribbed him a little for passing on the does and for getting lost.

The pair returned to their stands at 2 p.m. Just before dark, Fitzke heard leaves rustling behind him. He craned his ears. The sound was too light for cattle and it sounded like the animals were moving too fast for squirrels. He knew it had to be deer.

Soon two does jumped the fence, with eight more staying back. Fitzke raised his rifle to shoot, but the deer saw him moving, and all he had to look at was a bunch of white flags trotting off.

With time running out, he bleated a few times. Suddenly another faint sound came from where the does had been. Fitzke raised his rifle, just as a buck jumped the fence.

Fitzke shot, and thought he saw the buck stumble, then it was gone.

Putnam radioed Fitzke, and after hearing the story, rushed to his student's stand.

There were only a few drops of blood. The hunters searched, and seconds later, Putnam yelled for joy. The student was learning quickly judging by his beautiful 10-pointer.

10-Year-Old is on a Big-Buck Fast Track

Zach Eneix of Magnolia, Ohio, has killed two big bucks at a very young age.

After completing his hunter's safety course at age 8, Zach was ready to hunt in Fall 2001.

Zach and his father, Ron, had set up a ladder stand near a food plot. After much practice with his crossbow, Zach went on his first hunt, with Ron positioned in a climbing tree stand a few yards behind him.

On his first hunt, several does and a buck appeared, but the buck stayed just out of range.

Two days later, more does appeared, along with a 4-pointer. Then a bigger buck appeared. The small buck walked over to the does, and the big buck moved in to chase it away. Soon, the buck was a few feet from Zach's stand. Zach waited until he had a perfect shot before arrowing his first deer — a 12-pointer.

The following season, just after his 10th birthday, the rut was kicking in. Ron laid a scent trail, and after an hour of no activity, used a bleat call. As he put it away, Zach pointed out a fox squirrel, but there was more movement beyond the squirrel. A big buck approached.

HUNTER: **Zach Eneix**
DATE: **2001, 2002**
LOCATION: **Ohio**
METHOD: **Crossbow**
RACK: **12-point bucks**

The buck hit the scent trail and began lip curling. As it followed the trail, Zach aimed and made a quartering-away shot. The buck ran 35 yards and fell right in front of the young hunter's stand.

At 10 years old, Zach had already shot two 12-pointers. Neither he nor is father can wait for next season!

Ohio Boy Finds Buck Behind Family Cabin

Brad Buchanan of Hudson, Ohio, hoped his 11-year-old son, Brad Jr., would have a chance to shoot his first buck on opening day of Ohio's 2002 gun-deer season. The night before season opened, the pair headed to their cabin in Athens County.

Brad Sr. placed a double folding camp chair on a hill behind the cabin the night before the hunt. He hoped the spot would be a good one.

A half-hour before sunrise on opening morning, father and son made the short hike to the top of the hill. Brad Jr. toted a Remington 870 youth 20 gauge. Brad Sr. carried only a grunt call and some deer scent.

HUNTER: **Brad Buchanan**
DATE: **Opening Day 2002**
LOCATION: **Ohio**
METHOD: **Shotgun**
RACK: **8-point buck**

Brad Sr. hung a scent wick on a tree branch 30 yards from the setup, then both took their positions and awaited the dawn.

Squirrels became active about the time the first rays of light burned through the morning gray, making hearing difficult. However, 15 minutes into legal shooting time, Brad Sr. caught movement to his right. A nice buck was coming upwind right toward the scent!

Brad Sr. told his son to get ready because a buck was coming.

The younger Buchanan raised his shotgun, but the buck saw him move and bounded 20 yards downhill into thick slash.

The hunters thought they'd blown their chance, but even though the buck had spooked, they could still see it in the thicket below.

That's when Brad Sr. remembered the grunt call dangling from his neck. He blew two grunts and the buck immediately started walking downwind of him and his son. Buchanan blew twice more and the buck turned and came straight up the hill. Moments later, it was standing in the open 30 yards away.

Brad Jr. fired and the buck ran down the hill and out of sight. However, his shot was true and clipped the heart.

His first deer, an 8-pointer, had a 20-inch inside spread.

First Gun Buck is a Mesquite-Country Brute

Hunter McWaters of Virginia Beach, Va., developed an addiction to deer hunting at a young age. The first time he went bowhunting he developed the bug, and now, when he's not deer hunting, he's reading *Deer & Deer Hunting* magazine or watching deer hunting videos.

The young man learned of the large-antlered bucks of the Texas scrub country, and found out his father's friend owned part of a lease there.

HUNTER: **Hunter McWaters**
DATE: **Nov. 30, 2002**
LOCATION: **Texas**
METHOD: **.270 Rifle**
RACK: **8-point buck**

Before he knew it, McWaters and his father were off to the Mesquite Country of Texas on a combination turkey and deer hunt on the friend's lease.

The first evening McWaters bow-hunted, and though he had several deer within range, he couldn't get a shot.

Because he only had $2^1/_2$ days to hunt, and due to the open nature of the area, McWaters opted for a .270 on the first morning of his hunt.

McWaters was dropped off at a box blind. Before the sun was up, two 8-pointers and a 9-pointer appeared. McWaters thought about shooting one, but his father's friend told him there were plenty of big bucks around, so he waited.

A few minutes later McWaters saw a doe, and not far behind it was another 8-pointer. This buck was much larger than the ones he'd seen earlier, and he decided to shoot. The interesting thing is, he'd never shot a rifle bigger than a .22 before.

McWaters had to readjust his seat in the blind, and made noises that alerted the buck. The 8-pointer stared at the blind for a long time, but finally put its head down. Remembering what he had read about quartering-away shots, McWaters waited for a good angle before squeezing the trigger.

The buck dropped in its tracks, and McWaters happily walked over to his first buck shot with a rifle (he shot a buck with a bow a year earlier).

The 8-pointer field dressed at 155 pounds.

The next day McWaters bagged two gobblers on his successful Texas hunt.

Parade of Whitetails Ends with Big 8-Pointer

HUNTER: **Branden Budsberg**
DATE: **Sept. 28, 2002**
LOCATION: **Wisconsin**
METHOD: **Bow**
RACK: **8-point buck**

You can bet Branden Budsberg won't be giving up his bow-hunting spot any time soon.

Budsberg, of Amherst Junction, Wis., was hunting an oak grove 100 yards from a field edge Sept. 28, 2002. Using his climbing tree stand, he ascended a tree at about 2:45 p.m. on a warm, cloudy evening. Within 10 minutes, Budsberg began seeing deer.

Despite good deer activity, Budsberg didn't have any shot opportunities. Then, at 6:30, an 8-point buck appeared. It was the 21st deer he'd seen. It approached Budsberg at a trot, and apparently wanted to eat under the tree Budsberg was sitting in! The buck was only 5 yards away when Budsberg shot. The arrow hit the 180-pound 8-pointer in the spine, dropping it instantly.

Michigan Hunter Shoots Buck in First Season

HUNTER: **Brandon Denham**
DATE: **Oct. 28, 2000**
LOCATION: **St. Joe Co., Indiana**
METHOD: **Bow**
RACK: **8-point buck**

Brandon Denham of Niles, Mich., hopes future bow-seasons are like his first.

On Oct. 28, 2000, he planned to hunt in St. Joe County, Ind.

Things got off to a bad start. Denham didn't wake up until 8 a.m. He planned to be on stand long before that time, but decided to head out anyway.

It was sunny and warm, and it seemed everything was working against him.

After sitting in his stand for about 25 minutes, he blew a doe call a few times.

Within minutes, a buck appeared. Denham saw it coming, and when the buck ducked under a fence, Denham drew.

The buck stopped about 10 yards away, and Denham shot. The 8-pointer traveled only about 20 yards before piling up.

Grandmother Bags Buck On Her First Deer Hunt

Nova Ferguson, of Sycamore, Ohio, was not born into a hunting family. So when her husband, Tim, spent a good deal of his time raccoon hunting shortly after they were married in 1964, she wondered if Tim loved hunting and his dogs more than he loved her!

After 38 years of marriage, Ferguson learned many things about hunting, and soon her own sons were hooked on the sport. Finally, when her teenage grandsons shot their first deer, Ferguson decided to join them because deer hunting sounded easy.

HUNTER: **Nova Ferguson**
DATE: **Oct. 10, 2002**
LOCATION: **Ohio**
METHOD: **Crossbow**
RACK: **8-point buck**

So, after practicing all summer with a crossbow until she could consistently hit a bull's-eye, Ferguson went on her first hunt on Oct. 10, 2002. Ferguson's husband, Tim, and grandson, Jeremy, escorted her to her stand 16 feet up a tree on the edge of a wheat field. Then Tim went to his son, Craig's, house, and Jeremy went to his tree stand 300 yards away.

Ferguson's first thought as she sat alone on her stand for the first time was she hoped the fawns she'd watched grow up on the farm that summer wouldn't walk into range.

Soon after she sat down, she heard a noise to her right, and a red squirrel appeared. It wanted to climb the tree she was in, and she knew if it did, she would scream. Although she knew she wasn't supposed to leave human scent in the woods, she thought doing so would be better than screaming, so, forgetting her manners, she spit on the squirrel to scare it away!

After the squirrel episode, she settled down and waited. She sighted through the crossbow to make sure she could see clearly, and tried to estimate shooting distances. She also mentally reminded herself to push the safety off if a shot presented itself, remembering stories she'd heard in which this simple act had cost hunters a chance at a nice buck.

After about an hour and 20 minutes, she heard another noise, and although she'd never spent time alone in the woods, she knew this time it was a deer. Moments later, a buck stepped into the open about 30 feet away!

Ferguson pushed the safety, but it made a loud click and the buck froze. Ferguson stayed still, and after a few seconds, the deer settled down.

When the buck was a mere 12 feet from the base of the stand, Ferguson slowly raised the crossbow to her shoulder, but her jacket made a slight rustling noise, and the buck went on red alert.

Again, after a few seconds, the buck seemed to forget the noise and began smelling the ground where Ferguson had walked to get to her stand. Although the buck seemed unalarmed, Ferguson knew she had to act quickly.

She eased the scope to her eye. All she could see was deer hair. She found the buck's front legs, then the rear legs. When she was on the buck's vitals, she squeezed off a shot.

She knew it was a good shot, and the buck kicked up its heels and ran into the woods.

Ferguson couldn't believe she'd just shot a deer. What was even more unbelievable was the deer was a nice buck. It had all happened so fast, and she hadn't even hunted 1½ hours! Ferguson wasn't nervous — just very excited!

Ferguson knew she was supposed to wait 15 to 30 minutes before climbing down from her stand, but 5 minutes was all she could stand. She left the crossbow in her stand, then carefully descended.

Not knowing where the buck was, Ferguson sneaked quietly through the woods so she wouldn't disturb it if it was still alive. However, when she walked back to the trail, she saw it lying motionless in a field 150 yards from her stand.

Ferguson hurried home, but Tim wasn't there. She called Craig's house, and Craig's wife, Cheryl, handed Tim the phone. Tim couldn't believe that his wife had shot a buck, and Tim asked how big. In all her excitement, Ferguson hadn't really looked at the buck. She guessed maybe a small 5-pointer. Tim, Craig and Cheryl hurried back to the farm to see it.

As soon as Tim got to the house, he saw the buck lying in the distant field and knew it wasn't a small 5-pointer.

When everyone reached the deer, they were awed by Ferguson's buck. Jeremy heard the commotion and left his stand to investigate the source of all the excitement.

Ferguson's first buck was an 8-pointer with a 16-inch spread. It dressed at 170 pounds, and now Ferguson prides herself in being an official member of the Ferguson Buck Club. She hopes to shoot a bigger buck during her second season!

Mowing Lawns Leads to Teen's First Buck

The tale of Zach Sickmann's first deer hunt is an excerpt from the storybook of a different time.

Ever since he was old enough to listen to his father's and grandfather's stories, Zach had dreamed of hunting. He read outdoor magazines cover to cover and shot cans with his BB gun and .22 rifle. And his questions about guns were unending.

In the back of his mind, a dream to go deer hunting formed.

When he was 12, without telling anyone, he began saving money to buy a deer rifle. A few dollars from mowing lawns and from his allowance gradually blossomed into Zach's "gun fund."

Zach read more magazines, visited gun shops with his father, and asked the advice of his relatives before setting his mind on a Ruger .270. His relatives were proud of his decision.

Zach's interest in guns grew, and every time he visited his grandfather, he asked to clean the guns in the locked cabinet. His grandfather taught the young man the proper way to clean the firearms, and how to handle them responsibly.

On Christmas morning, 2001, Zach's gun fund went over the top. The next day Zach's father called the gun shop where a friend was holding a Ruger .270. Unfortunately, it had been sold.

HUNTER: **Zach Sickmann**
DATE: **December 2001**
LOCATION: **Texas**
METHOD: **.270 Rifle**
RACK: **7-point buck**

Only seven days remained in the Texas deer season. There was no time to order a gun, so Zach and his father found another gun shop. Zach bought his rifle, and the owner mounted and bore-sighted the scope he received from his uncle on Christmas morning. Soon it was time for Zach's first hunt.

Zach's uncle, Henry, and father, Tom, accompanied him to his blind. There was about two hours of shooting light left on the Mason County, Texas lease.

The overcast sky shielded the trio from the Texas heat while variable winds danced on their faces and necks.

As the light faded, Henry whispered encouragement to his nephew. It was time for action.

As dusk approached, Zach spotted a group of does about 200

yards away. A buck was with them. No one knew how big it was; only that it was big enough for a young man's first buck.

The deer moved closer as light waned. The buck stopped to drink at a pond 150 yards away.

Henry, the hunter in the family, struggled with what to say. He wanted to tell Zach enough so he'd know what to do, but time was running out.

"Should I shoot?" Zach asked.

"Yes, as soon as you can," Henry replied.

The fire from the rifle's muzzle blinded the hunters for a moment in the dim light after Zach touched the trigger. When their vision returned, the buck was on the ground.

After waiting a moment to make sure the deer was dead, father, son and uncle approached Zach's fallen deer. The dead buck was bigger than they imagined.

The buck's rack measured 23½ inches from beam to beam. And Zach, his father and uncle couldn't be happier.

Bad Start Leads to Sweet Ending

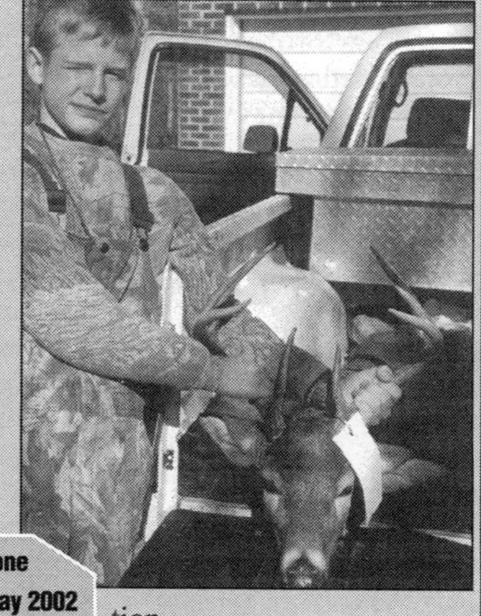

Opening morning of Tennessee's 2002 gun season got off to a bad start for Steven Stone of Allardt, Tenn. He got into the woods 15 minutes late, and didn't think he would see anything.

Luckily, his hunt wasn't doomed. At 7 a.m. Stone saw a doe about 140 yards away. It was coming up a ridge that Stone suspected deer traveled on. Stone hoped a buck would trail the doe, but there was nothing behind it.

HUNTER: **Steven Stone**
DATE: **Opening Day 2002**
LOCATION: **Tennessee**
METHOD: **.270 Rifle**
RACK: **8-point buck**

A half-hour later Stone saw a flash in the same place where he'd seen the doe earlier. This time he spotted two does running along the ridge, with a big buck behind them. The deer were about 140 yards away, but suddenly they turned and started running in Stone's direction.

When the buck was 30 yards away, Stone raised his .270 and fired. He hit the buck, but it stayed on its feet and ran right at Stone. When the buck was 10 yards away, Stone shot again and the deer dropped in its tracks.

Stone has killed nine deer, but the 8-pointer is his biggest yet.

Girl Kills Buck After Canceling Shopping Trip

HUNTER: **Sara Millerman**
DATE: **Dec. 1, 2002**
LOCATION: **Wisconsin**
METHOD: **.30-30 Rifle**
RACK: **150-class buck**

I have always wanted to go hunting with my dad and brothers. I was very excited when I finally got to go after I took my hunter safety course. We made a shack for our hunting camp and it was in our woods and all ready to go. I was pumped!

The first couple days of rifle-season, up until Thanksgiving, we hunted every day from sunup to sundown. I thought things would be more fun than what I was experiencing as I sat up in the stand, cold and trying not to fall asleep.

We took the day off of hunting for Thanksgiving, but were back out the next day. I was pretty excited because even though I hadn't seen anything yet, I still wanted every chance to get a deer.

That was the day my brother, Jeremy, shot his deer. He thought it was a doe, but it was a buck fawn. He was happy, even though it was a small deer. I teased him because it was small, but he just replied, "Yeah, you probably wish that you would have been there. At least I got a deer, and that is more than you can say."

I knew that he was right. That night my brother, Josh, and I spent the night in the hunting shack. We got up early and took a walk through our woods. On the other side of the woods from our shack, we started to see all of the buck rubs. Oh, how I wanted to get a buck, just so I could show up all of the guys in my grade and show them that I, being a girl, could beat them in one of the most manly sports out there.

That night my dad told me that one of the guys in my grade had shot a doe. I ended up talking to the boy that night, and he simply said, "Yeah, it's just a doe, nothing big. Did you go out and shoot the big one? Ha, ha!"

After that I was determined to shoot a buck. I didn't care about how big it was, as long as it was a buck so I could do better than him. Yet the next day, my sister, Amy, offered to take me shopping. I was going to go, just because I didn't feel like hunting, but my dad wanted me to have every chance I could to shoot a deer because he knew that's what I wanted to do.

So we went out for the last time that season, and I sat in a friend's deer stand in our woods and waited. By the time there was only one hour left of the season, I was so tired that I was playing with my doe-bleat can and singing my Spanish ABC's.

Then I heard something off to my right. I stopped and was suddenly alert, at least until I saw the blaze orange walking 75 yards in front of me. It was just one of my brothers doing the last drive of the season.

I continued to sing my ABC's when I heard another crash in front of me. When I looked u I saw a huge buck with enormous antlers trotting straight toward me!

I lifted my gun and took it off safety. I was shaking so badly that I thought that I would miss. All that was running through my head was, "I have to kill it! I have to be better than all the guys in my grade that think they are 'all that' when it comes to hunting! I have to get a bigger buck than Jeremy!"

The deer was about 45 yards away. I got the gun on my shoulder and slowly squeezed the trigger. I didn't feel a kick or hear the shot; all I was thinking about was the buck in front of me.

I saw the back of it drop, and it dragged itself for 20 yards. I reloaded, then the buck dropped for good.

I opened the bolt of my gun because I knew I couldn't crawl down the tree with it. I set it on the floor of my stand. Then I didn't know what to do. So I just started screaming, "It's huge! Hurry up, get over here! Wow, it's huge!"

Then I climbed out of my tree stand with my arms and legs waving all over, trying to find the handles and I was half way down when I heard something crashing through the woods and when I looked up, I saw that it was Josh. Jeremy was close behind him, and farther back was my dad, running full-speed at me.

Josh yelled, "Where is it? Where is it? Which way did it go? I hope we don't have to track it very far."

I screamed and pointed, "Right there, don't you see it? It's huge!"

As soon as Josh saw it, he stopped, then ran forward to see if it was dead.

We field dressed it and put it in the back of Josh's truck. As we drove home, cars started turning around and following us. By the time we got home there were about 15 people in the yard who wanted to hear the story.

When I went to school, none of the guys believed me and made me bring a picture to prove it. Some guys still think they had a larger buck than me, even though when they told me they had a lot of doubt in their voices. A lot of them think one of my brothers shot it, and I was just saying it was mine. Both my brothers say if they shot it, they wouldn't let me say it was mine.

A lot of people say that I will probably stop hunting now because I will never get a deer bigger than that, but I will continue hunting just for the pure joy and excitement of shooting a deer.

— SARA MILLERMAN, AGE 12

JOSEPH MARLOW of Merrillville, Ind., arrowed this 173-inch 11-pointer. Marlow had hunted the huge whitetail for four seasons.

3

Worth The Wait

Indiana Man Scores After Four-Year Quest

A chance sighting during Indiana's 1997 shotgun deer season led a bow-hunter on a four-year hunt for a monster whitetail. In 2001, Joe Marlow, of Merrillville, Ind., bagged his trophy.

Hunting this deer became almost an obsession for Marlow. He scouted hard every season to learn the buck's movement patterns. He bought a Scent-Lok suit and vowed to only hunt his stand when the wind was in his favor .

Marlow made the extra effort to ensure he wouldn't disturb the buck as he walked to and from his tree stand, also, walking twice as far as the most direct route. Marlow had done his homework. It was from this stand that he intended to wait out the monster whitetail.

Marlow's long wait ended during the first weekend of November 2001 during Indiana's bow-season.

Marlow hunted the stand for the fourth time that season that week-end, and like his previous sits, his morning hunt yielded no sign of the big buck. However, Marlow was determined to stick it out, and stayed in his stand. The idea paid off. At about 4 p.m., Marlow raised his binoculars and saw the buck cutting across a distant bean field.

The buck was heading in his direction, and had apparently picked up the scent trail that Marlow had lain earlier. Marlow grunted, then lost sight of the buck.

Time crawled by as Marlow anxiously waited for the buck to reappear. Finally, after a few agonizing minutes, Marlow caught a glimpse of the buck, which was still working its way in his direction.

The buck closed the distance to 40 yards, and Marlow drew his bow. When the buck stood broad-side at 17 yards, Marlow had the opportunity he'd awaited for four years. He took careful aim and released his arrow.

The buck jumped a little at the shot, then trotted off as if it hadn't been hit, but Marlow knew he'd made a good shot. The heart-shot buck piled up after traveling only 50 yards.

Marlow's huge 11-point white-tail measured 173 Boone and Crockett inches.

Hunter Makes Good On 45-Year Promise

HUNTER: **Dale Schrope**
DATE: **Nov. 6, 2001**
LOCATION: **Pennsylvania**
METHOD: **Bow**
RACK: **18-point buck**

In 1956, Dale Schrope of Jersey Shore, Pa., grew interested in deer hunting. He saved money from his paper route and purchased a Stevens 12 gauge side-by-side shotgun.

The old gun's bead was broken off, and the owner had replaced it with a small die from a card game.

That fall, Schrope sat on a stump on his father's farm on opening morning of Pennsylvania's buck season. By 10 a.m., he had seen nothing, when suddenly a 10-point buck with a 2-foot spread approached to within 30 yards. Schrope emptied both barrels on the buck, reloaded, and shot twice more. None of the pumpkin balls connected.

Schrope looked to the sky and made a promise that he would pursue whitetails until he died.

Forty-five years later in 2001, Schrope's equipment had changed, but his quest for a big buck hadn't. Schrope had patiently awaited his second chance at a big buck. It came on Nov. 6.

Schrope had just finished a mile hike up a semi-dry creek bed. To the west was a clover field with five deer in it, two of which were bucks.

Suddenly, the larger buck chased one of the does toward Schrope. They passed him at about 30 yards. Schrope drew but couldn't shoot. Then he heard leaves rustling behind him, and when he looked, the other buck was chasing a doe.

In the next 15 minutes, a buck chased a doe past Schrope four times, and although Schrope drew every time, he couldn't get a shot.

Finally, Schrope heard a limb crack, and saw a doe with a buck trailing 20 yards behind her. They were heading for an opening about 40 yards away. Schrope drew, and, using his 30-yard sight pin, held high on the buck and released.

The buck fell, then got up and ran awkwardly about 45 yards into a briar patch and bedded down.

Schrope waited an hour and a half before leaving, then picked up his hunting partner. After eating and changing clothes, they returned. They found no blood where the deer was when Schrope shot, so they walked to the briar patch. The buck, which Schrope thought was an 8-pointer, was there, but it wasn't an 8-pointer, but rather, an 18-pointer! The buck dressed at about 230 pounds and was the biggest either hunter had ever seen.

Schrope's wife asked if his quest was finally over.

He looked at her, smiled, and said, "It's just begun."

Bow-Hunter Waits 20 Years for His Buck

Every year for 20 years, Frank Gongloff of Kingstowne, Va., and his hunting partners hunted in Pennsylvania, and every year, he went home skunked. In 2001, for the first time, it bothered him.

While on a week-long hunt, Gongloff looked skyward and asked for a sign to keep hunting. Minutes later, a forkhorn passed his stand, but it was too far. It wasn't the sign Gongloff wanted.

HUNTER: **Frank Gongloff**
DATE: **2001**
LOCATION: **Pennsylvania**
METHOD: **Bow**
RACK: **13-point buck**

Three days of swirling winds complicated the hunt. The deer weren't moving because they couldn't rely on their noses. Frustrated, Gongloff decided to pack up and end his hunt a day early.

Before he left, his brother pulled up ready to hunt. The winds had died down and his brother's theory that the deer would be moving after three days of laying idle was all the arm twisting Gongloff needed for one more evening hunt.

As Gongloff and his brother set out for a cornfield, they walked past two apple trees with a scrape underneath. The apple trees were in a natural funnel created by two drainage ditches. Gongloff decided a nearby oak looked like a great place to set up.

Gongloff had been sitting for quite a while when he heard a buck rubbing a tree. Seconds later he saw legs coming, then the buck emerged.

Gongloff tried to draw, but the buck stopped to test the wind. He drew when the buck stepped behind a small oak 18 yards away.

The buck took its time, munching acorns while it was obstructed. Finally, it inched its way past the oak, but its shoulder was back. Finally it stepped forward, and Gongloff touched his release.

When he climbed down, he couldn't find blood or his arrow. He met his brother at the edge of a cornfield, and when they returned, they found blood 15 yards from where the buck had stood when Gongloff shot.

They dumped their gear off at the truck and returned a half-hour later and found a good blood trail. They found Gongloff's 13-pointer dead at the bottom of a hill.

The buck was an incredible trophy for Gongloff, but every time he looks at the buck on his wall, he remembers the memories he gets from deer hunting, which, to him, is the real trophy.

Thoughts of Moving Dashed by 10-Pointer

Tony Marascio of Dublin, Ohio, was frustrated with his hunting land. After four years of intensively hunting the area, he and his hunting partner had only filled one deer tag.

What's worse, they now hunted on the ground after several of their tree stands mysteriously disappeared.

However, the hunters had seen two different trophy bucks and just enough deer sign to keep them from pulling anchor. But the longer they hunted without getting a shot at a trophy buck, the greener other pastures appeared.

HUNTER: **Tony Marascio**
DATE: **Nov. 15, 2002**
LOCATION: **Ohio**
METHOD: **Bow**
RACK: **10-point buck**

Things changed for the better on Nov. 15, 2002. Marascio awoke late that morning, so he didn't reach his stand until 6:45 a.m. He was stationed downwind of a doe bedding area, so he was optimistic for the morning's hunt.

As the sun slowly rose, Marascio saw his hunting partners walking across the field in front of him. He waited until they disappeared from sight, then gave three hard blows on his grunt tube.

About 10 minutes later, Marascio turned to his left and couldn't believe his eyes. He spotted a big 10-point buck standing on a nearby ridge. The buck was walking toward a scrape where Marascio had seen a small 8-point buck the day before.

When the 10-pointer stepped into Marascio's shooting lane 9 yards away, Marascio released his arrow.

The buck dropped to its front knees, then recovered and bolted into the field.

Marascio sat motionless and in awe as the big buck dashed across the field.

Marascio recovered the buck about 150 yards from where he hit it.

When Marascio looked at his watch, he noticed that only 25 minutes had passed since he entered his stand.

After recovering his 10-pointer, all Marascio's thoughts of finding a new hunting area were laid to rest.

Marascio's 10-point Ohio whitetail field dressed at 220 pounds.

Tes Randle Jolly
Alabama, 1999
11-pointer

Tes Randle Jolly

Camera Helps Hunter Hunt Harder, Longer

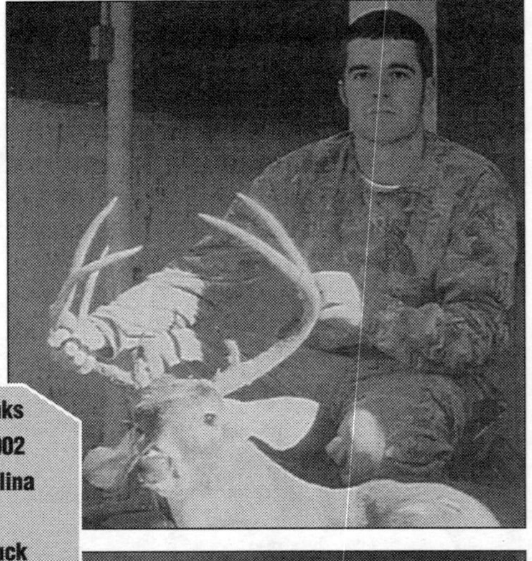

HUNTER: **Danny Blanks**
DATE: **Nov. 29, 2002**
LOCATION: **South Carolina**
METHOD: **.243 Rifle**
RACK: **10-point buck**

Sometimes it can be tough to stay on stand hour after hour, day after day. But when you know there's a big 10-pointer in your area, it becomes a little easier to stick with it.

Danny Blanks of Fort Mill, S.C., learned that in 2002. He had put out a remote-sensing camera, and the pictures he got surprised him. He recorded a half-dozen pictures of a big 10-pointer on his hunting land. Friends who saw the photos said it was the biggest buck they'd seen in the area in a long time.

Blanks made it a goal to tag the big 10-pointer. Blanks saw the buck twice during bow-season, but couldn't get a good shot at the buck. As the season wore on, he thought about shooting other deer, but decided to hold out for the big boy. No one had shot the buck, so he knew it still had to be out there.

By late November, still no one had gotten the buck.

On Nov. 29, now equipped with his .243, Blanks went afield. Blanks hunted the same area where he'd gotten the big buck's picture.

Early that morning, Blanks grunted a couple times, and the big 10-pointer responded. The buck came in within 25 yards, and with a well-placed shot, Blanks' hunt was over.

Blanks' 10-pointer weighed 195 pounds.

33-Hour Drive Proves Worthwhile

Spencer Prescott of Columbiaville, Mich., is a dedicated deer hunter. He must be, because in October 2002, he spent 33 hours in the back seat of a pickup truck driving from his Michigan home to his deer hunting destination in Saskatchewan!

Prescott and five other hunters booked a hunt during Saskatchewan's October primitive weapons hunt. The group arrived on a Saturday evening, but because Sunday hunting is not permitted, they couldn't hunt until Monday. The hunters spent Sunday scouting for bucks.

HUNTER: **Spencer Prescott**
DATE: **October 2002**
LOCATION: **Saskatchewan**
METHOD: **Muzzleloader**
RACK: **14-point buck**

Early Monday morning, Prescott was in his stand, which consisted of a box in a tree with windows on each side.

The morning was cold and crisp, and Prescott saw early action. He videotaped a small 8-pointer and saw does, fawns and small bucks all morning.

About noon, two does walked under Prescott's stand and intently watched their back trail. Prescott swung his video camera, and the viewfinder filled with a 10-point buck with mahogany antlers and a 20-inch spread!

However, Prescott couldn't shoot. The buck was too far to the right to maneuver his muzzleloader into the small window, and with the does directly below him, he risked spooking the deer.

After 5 long minutes, Prescott slowly poked the rifle barrel out the window. Just then, Prescott heard an ATV, and the deer bolted!

That night, Prescott told his guide he wanted a different stand. The guide looked at the video footage of the big buck and said he should stay put. Besides, the guide told him the ATV incident was a fluke, and most deer in the area had never seen a human.

Prescott returned even earlier the next morning. About 7 a.m. he heard a deer walking. He picked up his binoculars and counted seven points on one side!

Again Prescott struggled to poke the barrel out the window, but soon his cross hairs were centered on the buck's shoulder. He said a quick prayer and fired. The buck leaped 20 feet, then disappeared. Prescott thought he'd missed, but when he climbed down he found the buck dead 40 feet away. The 14-pointer field dressed at 215 pounds.

Long-Time Bow-Hunter Gets Anniversary Gift

Mike Potenza of Southampton, Mass., celebrated his 40th year of hunting in 1999. He began bow hunting with a lemonwood bow at age 12, and though his equipment has changed considerably over four decades, he still holds the same enjoyment for deer hunting.

On Sept. 18, 1999, Potenza headed to his bow stand in neighboring Connecticut for an afternoon hunt. It was 85 degrees, but Potenza preferred the heat over a late-season hunt in which the temperature had been 8 degrees below zero. Potenza wiped the sweat with scent wipes and eased back for a long sit.

HUNTER: **Mike Potenza**
DATE: **Sept. 18, 1999**
LOCATION: **Connecticut**
METHOD: **Bow**
RACK: **8-point buck**

Potenza assumed there would be no action for a long while because it was early and hot, and most deer wouldn't move until evening. Potenza's mind drifted back to small-game hunts on the family farm in New Jersey, now 40-plus years gone by.

Hunting was popular in the area, and schools even closed for the opening day of deer season. On the small-game hunts, the whole family would gather at the farm the night before, and the evening was filled with food, jokes and fun. In the morning, the men awoke to a fine breakfast that the women prepared, then set off. As a child, Potenza tagged along with his father and uncle, and his job was to find downed game and carry it. It made him feel like he was part of the hunt, and it made him long for the days when he would be old enough to carry a gun afield.

His daydreaming was interrupted by a flicker of motion 40 yards away. Just when he started to doubt that he'd seen anything, Potenza saw movement again. He thought it was too early in the afternoon to be a deer, but a deer it was!

Thinking it was probably just a yearling, Potenza looked away from the deer, but when he saw antlers, his attention became fixed on the buck.

Potenza slowly stood and lifted his bow from the holder. The buck was in heavy cover, but eventually stepped into an opening where it fed on acorns. Just when Potenza thought the buck was going to leave, it began walking down a trail toward him!

The 8-point buck was closing fast when Potenza saw a larger 10-pointer behind the 8-pointer. Now Potenza faced a real dilemma!

Potenza decided to take the first good shot he was offered.

Things seemed to go in slow motion, and when the 8-pointer stopped behind a small tree, Potenza drew. The 8-pointer stopped broadside 15 yards away. Potenza remembers placing his sight pin behind the front shoulder, but has no recollection of touching off his release. But he heard the arrow hit the buck, and the 8-pointer ran off. The 10-pointer, sensing something wasn't right, slowly turned and walked away.

It took Potenza a moment to realize what had just transpired, and when it sunk in, Potenza's legs turned to Jell-o, and he flopped down in his seat. He was shaking so much he had a hard time putting his bow back in its holder.

Potenza waited an hour before climbing down from his stand to look for the deer. He found nothing at first, then 30 yards from where the buck stood, he found 10 inches of broken arrow and a good blood trail. After following the trail for about 80 yards, Potenza jumped the buck. He decided to end the search and look for the deer the next morning.

The 1½-hour drive home gave Potenza plenty of time to think about the details of his hunt. He didn't get home until midnight, and without thinking about what time it was, he called his friend, Dale Johnson, to tell his story, much to Dale's wife's disliking. Johnson told Potenza to calm down. Johnson's wife told him to shut up!

Johnson said he'd ask his boss for the morning off, and Johnson's boss (who was also a friend of Potenza's) was so excited, he asked to come along to search for Potenza's deer. Excitement filled the 1½-hour drive back to Connecticut.

The men picked up the blood trail, and when it ran out, each man followed a different deer trail. Potenza searched on his hands and knees and was rewarded when he found a pinhead-sized drop of blood. Potenza kept crawling while Smith went ahead.

"Hey, Mike, here's your deer," Smith shouted.

Potenza ran ahead to see.

"That's a rock," Potenza replied.

"I don't think rocks have horns," Smith answered.

Potenza was looking in the wrong spot. Indeed, Potenza's buck was laying up ahead, dead.

Potenza shot his biggest buck with a bow on his 40th anniversary of hunting, and had the pleasure of spending it with good friends.

Wyoming Hunt Produces Buck of a Lifetime

Lester Arnold of Jonestown, Pa., and his son have hunted whitetails together for almost 20 years. Over the years, each hunter had shot several bucks and does, and both enjoy each other's company while hunting. But something was always missing from their hunts: a once-in-a-lifetime trophy buck.

To fill the void, Arnold and his son, Brent, began going on out-of-state hunting trips in pursuit of a wall-hanger buck. However, each hunt only resulted in disappointment.

HUNTER: **Lester Arnold**
DATE: **Nov. 26, 2001**
LOCATION: **Wyoming**
METHOD: **Gun**
RACK: **13-point buck**

In 2000, they got serious about setting up their dream hunt.

They researched outfitters and sought recommendations. After poring over their findings, they booked a hunt in Wyoming for the 2001 season.

Lester and Brent had plenty of time to prepare for the hunt, and they gathered their gear, shot a lot of targets and did everything they could to ensure success on their hunt.

When the trip finally arrived, they flew from Harrisburg, Pa., to Rapid City, S.D., and went to Mt. Rushmore, Devil's Tower and Spearfish Canyon before traveling to Wyoming for their five-day hunt.

The first morning both hunters saw several average and large bucks, but they were too far to shoot. In the afternoon, Lester went with the guide, and Brent hunted by himself. Brent saw seven bucks that evening, but didn't fire a shot. When darkness overcame him, he could do nothing but wait for the guide to pick him up.

After waiting for an hour after dark in minus 10-degree weather, the guide and Lester finally arrived. When the truck pulled up, Brent saw a huge set of antlers in the box!

Lester had bagged a 13-point whitetail with three sticker points — his best buck ever. It brought the kid out of the 57-year-old hunter, and the Arnolds threw a major celebration.

They are now planning a caribou hunting adventure. No matter what the outcome of their trips, they always enjoy the time spent together and the memories of their hunts.

New York Hunter Fondly Remembers 2002

Jim Eichinger of Kenmore, N.Y., will always remember the 2002 hunting season. After 22 years of hunting, he shot his first buck.

Eichinger began bow-hunting five years ago. Last season, he equipped himself with a new bow and practiced frequently.

Deer were everywhere on opening weekend. Bucks browsed for acorns, chased does and a button buck even napped yards from Eichinger's stand. A 6-pointer walked within 15 yards, but Eichinger didn't have a shot.

As the season progressed, Eichinger pored over his logbook from previous years, trying everything to get a feel for what deer might be doing and how best to take advantage of his information.

HUNTER: **Jim Eichinger**
DATE: **Nov. 4, 2002**
LOCATION: **New York**
METHOD: **Bow**
RACK: **8-point buck**

On Nov. 3, things got rolling. A nice buck appeared 30 yards away — mere feet from a trail camera Eichinger had set up earlier that day.

Eichinger drew, took a few deep breaths and released his arrow. He waited an hour after his shot before climbing down from his stand, and after thoroughly scouring the area and finding his arrow, he realized he missed.

Eichinger was dejected and began questioning himself. "What if I'd waited longer?" he thought. His friend convinced him not to give up, and the next day Eichinger returned to the same stand.

After an hour, four legs appeared in a nearby valley. Finally, an off-white rack appeared.

Eichinger grunted twice, and the buck began heading his way. The buck scraped the snow, worked a licking branch and eventually found Eichinger's scent trail. The buck followed the trail, and when it was 12 yards away, Eichinger shot. The deer bounded off and fell 60 yards away. After 22 years of waiting, Eichinger was rewarded with an 8-point buck.

Ohio Hunter's First Buck Is One for the Books

Josh Dennison of Apple Creek, Ohio, has a perfect bow-hunter's schedule. His work shift is from 7:30 p.m. to 4:30 a.m., allowing him to hunt mornings and afternoons.

On Nov. 5, 2001, Dennison headed to the woods after working his shift all night.

A deer snorted and bounded off in darkness as he got out of his truck. Dennison quickly donned his bow-hunting apparel, checked over his equipment and headed into the inky blackness of the woods.

HUNTER: **Josh Dennison**
DATE: **Nov. 5, 2001**
LOCATION: **Ohio**
METHOD: **Bow**
RACK: **20-point buck 160-class**

He stopped periodically to prevent himself from working up a sweat, check the wind and listen. He spooked two more deer on the way to his river bottom stand site, but there was nothing he could do about it, and he continued on.

Dennison reached his stand site, about 70 yards from a bedding area. It was one of the few trees that was straight enough or big enough to hold his climbing stand.

After settling down, he dipped a stick in some doe estrous scent and tossed it a reasonable shooting distance from his tree. Then he bleated three times, grunted twice and sat back to watch the day begin.

Only a couple minutes had passed when Dennison heard something to his left. He picked up his bow and got ready. When he turned his head in the sound's direction, he almost fell out of his tree. A huge buck was trotting toward him.

Dennison told himself not to blow the opportunity.

When the buck was 20 yards away, it let out a deep grunt, then turned left, presenting a 15-yard broadside shot.

As Dennison shook his bow into position, the buck stopped to smell the doe-in-estrus scent Dennison had tossed on the ground.

Dennison peered through his peep and found his pin, but the size of the monster buck's rack rattled him to no end. As Dennison squeezed the trigger on his release, the buck whirled and bolted.

Dennison's heart sank when the buck slowed and he realized his shot was too far back. Dennison waited a long time before climbing down from his stand to follow the buck's blood trail.

When he finally took up the blood trail, to his amazement, the trail was quite heavy and easy to follow. As Dennison approached the bedding area, however, the trail grew thinner. When Dennison looked ahead, he looked right into the eyes of the wounded buck.

Before Dennison could draw his bow, the buck picked itself up from its bed and ran blindly through the thick underbrush. Dennison was left with only a mental image of saplings bending to the ground as the buck hauled its massive headgear through the thicket.

Dennison knew he had to back off and let time take its toll on the deer. As he walked back to his truck, the best and worse scenarios ran through his head. In 10 years of hunting, Dennison had shot does, but never a buck. He did not want his first buck to get away.

After discussing the situation, his girlfriend, Kristen, and brother, Justin, decided to come along to help him find his trophy buck.

Justin stationed himself at the far end of the bedding area, and Kristen and Dennison took up the blood trail. When the trackers reached the spot where Dennison had last seen the buck, they saw it again. It bounded away, and they retreated and decided to postpone the search until the following morning.

It was an uneasy night at work for Dennison, and time crawled by. Finally, when he got out of work, he met up with Kristen and they returned to the bottomland forest. Justin couldn't come because of school, so Kristen posted on the other side of the bedding area.

Just as they got ready to start the search, Dennison noticed something out of place, and soon a deer bolted from Kristen's direction. Luckily it was just a doe, and not the big buck, as Dennison feared.

After just a few steps along the blood trail, Dennison saw the buck. This time, however, it was lifeless and laying on the ground under a brush pile. A quick check revealed that indeed the buck was dead, and Dennison's long wait for his first buck was over, and he let out a shout of excitement and relief.

Dennison dragged the monster whitetail into the open, where Kristen helped him field dress the buck, then the pair struggled to load all 220 pounds of buck into Dennison's pickup before heading home to make phone calls and show off his impressive first buck!

Dennison's buck sported 20 points and was shot exactly one month before his 20th birthday. The buck had a 21 1/2-inch inside spread and scored 160 4/8 nontypical inches, qualifying for the Ohio Buckeye Big Buck Club. The buck was estimated at 3 1/2 years old.

Gary Sefton, November 2002
8-pointer, southern Illinois

Hunter Matches Wits With Tall 9-Point Buck

Tom Bishop of Elon, N.C., saw a 9-point buck during North Carolina's 2002 bow-season. He decided to exclusively hunt this deer. However, tracking down the elusive 9-pointer was no easy task.

During the remainder of bow-season, Bishop hunted from several different stands, but didn't see the tall-tined 9-point buck again.

Finally, on the second-to-last day of muzzleloader season, Bishop got a brief glimpse of the buck — from the same stand he'd first seen it.

HUNTER: **Tom Bishop**
DATE: **2002**
LOCATION: **North Carolina**
METHOD: **Muzzleloader**
RACK: **9-point buck**

The next day Bishop knew he had to hunt aggressively if he hoped to shoot the buck before hunters flooded the woods during gun season, which opened the following day. Bishop decided to hang a stand in the buck's bedding area.

Bishop slipped into a dense honeysuckle thicket, moving so slowly and cautiously his muscles ached. After quickly hanging the tree stand, he quietly slipped out of the thicket.

Bishop returned to the stand 2½ hours later for his evening hunt. The area was littered with scrapes, rubs, tracks and droppings, and he hoped the buck would move through the area in search of does.

At about 5 p.m., Bishop heard a deer coming toward him along a creek bottom. When it appeared 45 yards away, it had its head down. After crossing a log, Bishop saw that it was the 9-pointer!

Bishop wanted to shoot right away, but he knew the buck was unalarmed, so he waited until the buck walked closer.

When the buck was 35 yards away, it turned to its right, giving Bishop a broadside shot. Bishop aimed behind the shoulder and fired. His shot was true, and the buck ran only 20 yards before dropping.

The 9-pointer that Bishop worked so hard for is his biggest buck ever.

Ironically, Bishop hunted from the same tree stand several more times during the gun-season but didn't see a single deer from the stand.

Man Ends Dry Run, Bonds With Family

A big buck nicknamed "Bullwinkle" brought three generations of Wisconsin hunters together in 2001.

Marty Jacobs and his son, Ken, bought 25 acres of hunting land in 1998. Along with Marty's father, Ed, the men set up deer camp every year. For several years, they knew a big buck was roaming the property. They found half its rack in spring 1999, and both sheds in 2001.

However, hunting hadn't been good, and after a few years, the Jacobs were thinking about selling the property. Fortunately, Marty shot a 9-pointer in 2000, which renewed interest in hunting the area.

HUNTER: **Ed Jacobs**
DATE: **2001**
LOCATION: **Wisconsin**
METHOD: **Gun**
RACK: **13-point buck**

Things worked out for the best in 2001. Ed was hunting from a ground blind during the season. He hadn't shot a buck since 1972.

Bullwinkle appeared, and Ed fired one shot at it. The buck ran off and crossed a highway.

Thinking he'd missed, Ed was disgruntled. He was done hunting for the season.

As the party searched for the buck, however, Marty found kicked-up gravel where the buck had crossed the highway, and soon Ken found a speck of blood.

After that, Ken found the dead buck 150 yards from Ed's ground blind.

Ken raced to get his grandfather, blurting "Wait till you see it!"

Ed's first buck in 29 years was truly a memorable one. The gray-muzzled 13-pointer was about $5^1/_2$ years old. It dressed out at 185 pounds.

But the unity of the hunt was far more important than shooting Bullwinkle. Hunting together has drawn Ed and Marty closer, after not seeing eye to eye for a few years.

There are now no plans of selling the hunting land. The only plan is for the head mount of Bullwinkle to grace the wall of the cabin the Jacobs intend to build.

Hunter's First Buck Is 15 Years in the Making

Sometimes success takes patience.

Chaun Bergsma of Sault Sainte Marie, Mich., didn't grow up hunting. But his uncle Mark taught him how to hunt, and in 1988, Bergsma bought his first deer license.

In the first 20 minutes of his first still-hunt, Bergsma missed a nice buck. He didn't shoot at another deer until the 2002 season.

On Nov. 18, 2002, Bergsma was the only hunter at the Triple "B" deer camp. He awoke, started a fire and ate breakfast, and considered not hunting so he wouldn't disturb the woods as he waited for his companions to arrive. However, he decided a morning hunt couldn't hurt, and if nothing else, he could enjoy watching the swamp awaken.

HUNTER: **Chaun Bergsma**
DATE: **Nov. 18, 2002**
LOCATION: **Michigan**
METHOD: **.300 Win. Mag. Rifle**
RACK: **8-point buck**

At 7 a.m., Bergsma was hunting from the Southwest Seat and all was quiet, until he heard hoof steps. Twenty minutes passed, and Bergsma had almost forgotten about the noise when he heard a twig snap loudly.

Bergsma slowly and quietly raised his rifle and waited for the animal to move again.

He glanced left for a moment, and when he looked back to the source of the noise, a nice buck was standing in the trail 100 yards away.

Bergsma shouldered his .300 Win. Mag., aligned the cross hairs on the buck's boiler room and fired.

The buck crashed through the alders briefly, and came to a halt with a loud crash.

Bergsma returned to camp to ready himself for an all-day drag, if necessary. When he returned to his deer stand, he found blood and hair where the buck was standing when he shot.

Bergsma followed a good blood trail, but then lost it. However, a quick circle led Bergsma to the buck only 70 yards from where he'd shot it.

Bergsma's 8-point swamp buck dressed out at 175 pounds. Not only was it his first buck, it was the first deer he'd shot at since his first day of deer hunting 15 years earlier.

Third Year is Lucky

It was two years ago, in the last week of deer hunting season when I saw him. He was a monster, with the largest set of antlers I had seen in my 20 years of deer hunting.

My son John and I had been hunting together for the past five years, with both of us usually getting a deer. We all called John the "buck man" as he almost always connects with a buck. The last two years he got an 8-pointer each year, with the last one being exceptionally large.

HUNTERS: **Charles Craven, John Craven**
DATE: **1986**
LOCATION: **New Brunswick**
METHOD: **Gun**
RACK: **13-point buck, 8-point buck**

I know that hunting is 80 percent luck, but he got those bucks because he scouted the area very well before setting up a blind on some deer runways.

Two years ago, while scouting the area, John found a line of fresh scrapes. He and I built a tree blind overlooking some runways which were close to the line of scrapes.

The first morning of season, John was sitting in his blind at 7:30 a.m., and 30 minutes later a nice 8-pointer came by to check its scrapes, and John shot him with his .308.

Meanwhile, for the next two weeks I saw only white tails running through the trees. Finally, I thought I would try John's tree blind.

The next few days were very windy, and heavy rains kept many hunters home. On the last day of hunting season, the cold weather came. I was up well before daylight and proceeded to the blind in semi-darkness. Arriving at the stand, I pulled on an extra sweater that I had carried in with me, as I knew it would be bitterly cold sitting in a tree for several hours.

The sun finally came up, and the birds and animals of the forest came alive.

Anyone who has not hunted from a blind does not realize what they are missing. I have had birds land on branches within a foot of me, staring at me eye to eye. Squirrels have run over my hands as I rested them on tree trunks or branches. At the bottom of the tree, I have dropped pieces of sandwiches to the ground and watched squirrels, birds, field mice and even a marten share my lunch.

On the last day of the season, I waited and waited and got colder and colder. I stayed in my stand until about 4 p.m. and was about ready to leave when a sharp crack brought my heart to my mouth. The trouble was, the crack was behind me instead of on the regular runway in front of me. I turned my head ever so slowly, and there, not 30 feet away, was a monster buck.

He was to the right of me and slightly behind, and if I had been a left-handed shot, I might have had a chance at him. He was spooked and kept looking at the bottom of the tree stand. I guess my scent was there. Anyway, he knew something was not right. I counted his points and he was a beautiful 10-pointer. He turned on a dime and took off into the forest behind me.

Even though I did not get him, just seeing him eye to eye made my hunting season.

Last season I saw him only once. He was running through the trees. I had to settle for a spikehorn, while John bagged a 7-pointer.

This year (1986) there was a lot of lumbering and other activity going on, so we were not so successful in the early part of the season. However, during the last week, John got an 8-pointer on Wednesday at around 4 p.m. The next morning before first light I was out. I planned a hunt in an area where we had seen many deer signs. As I got to the spot, I was disappointed to find another hunter already there. Little did I know that it was a blessing in disguise.

Different hunting spots ran through my mind, and I settled on our old tree blind, where I had seen the monster buck two years in a row.

As I reached the blind, a doe ran across the path ahead of me. As I climbed the tree, I thought of the big buck who was king of the mountain around here. I settled in for a long wait, but just 45 minutes in, a loud crack sent my heart to my mouth again. It was the big buck, and he was following the doe.

This time he came across in front of me, and I settled the cross hairs on his chest. As I squeezed the trigger, I thought that he seemed much bigger than he was two years before. My shot was true, and he ran for 50 yards and fell in a heap.

I climbed down from the blind with my heart still pounding. Much to my surprise, he was now a 13-pointer, with six points on the left side and seven on the right.

It took me three years to get this trophy, and that's why I'm calling this story "Third Year is Lucky."

— Charles Craven

DAVID LANGE of Newfane, N.Y., shot "the big one" on Nov. 27, 2001. His drop-tine buck had an 18-inch spread and an 8-inch drop tine.

4

My Best Buck

Prophetic N.Y. Hunter Tags 'The Big One'

David Lange of Newfane, N.Y., didn't have as much time to bowhunt as usual during the 2001 bow season, due to the birth of his daughter. However, he made up for lost hunting time in a big way when he managed to get out a bit during the firearms season.

On Nov. 27, he got home from work early and decided to go hunting. He told his family he was going to get "the big one" as he walked out the door. Although his family laughed at him, his words proved prophetic.

Armed with his scoped .30-30 pistol, he walked into the woods toward his stand on a wood pile. On the way, he saw movement in a goldenrod field. Two does in the field saw him and ran into the woods, followed by a monster buck.

After spooking the deer, Lange quickly changed his plans and sneaked down a logging road to a food plot downwind of the deer. He decided to sit there until dark.

Fifteen minutes later two does and a small buck entered the food plot. Lange was about to shoot the small buck when he caught movement in some adjacent pines. It was the big buck!

The buck was 170 yards away and nervous, but it saw the other deer and cautiously fed toward them.

Lange was shaking so bad he couldn't hold his gun up. He crept to a big tree with a low limb for a rest.

The big buck was now about 120 yards away. Lange told himself to take his time and squeeze the trigger. When he had the cross hairs on the buck's shoulder, he touched off a round. The buck dropped.

Lange thanked the Lord, then ran to the fallen buck, which was still kicking. A second shot finished the deer.

Lange called home and explained that he would be late because he shot "the big one." His family was doubtful, having heard that story before. But when he got home, Lange's family was impressed with the buck and the fact that he had followed through on what he said he was going to do.

The buck sported an 18-inch spread and an 8-inch drop tine. It weighed 168 pounds field dressed and is Lange's biggest buck in 16 years of hunting.

South Dakota Bucks Impress Eastern Hunter

HUNTER: **Mike Caldarelli**
DATE: **Nov. 10, 2002**
LOCATION: **South Dakota**
METHOD: **Gun**
RACK: **10-point buck**

Occasional snowflakes fell from the wide-reaching steel-gray sky. The heavy winds that had buffeted the South Dakota prairie earlier that morning had subsided and were replaced by a dead calm. I had been sitting in an elevated box blind for about an hour that afternoon and had yet to see a deer.

It was Nov. 10, 2002, and I was anxious to see some of the large, rut-crazed bucks I'd learned inhabited south-central South Dakota.

My stand was situated 200 yards off a large alfalfa field and overlooked a wide, steep ravine. Pockets of open grasslands, some a few yards wide, others expansive, broke the thick scrub oak covering the hills around the stand.

At 4 p.m., I noticed movement in the brush about 300 yards across the ravine. I raised my binoculars and spotted the rear half of a deer vanishing into the brush. The deer's tail had been held straight out from its body, parallel to the ground. Even at that distance, I could see the deer was huge.

The thick brush completely concealed the deer. I anxiously watched the hillside, trying to detect any sign of the big whitetail.

After about five minutes, a deer stepped out into a small opening 200 yards directly across the ravine. A lone oak tree in the clearing obscured the deer's head. Through my scope, I could tell this was one of the largest deer I had ever seen.

Although I could not see antlers, I was certain the deer was a buck. I realized that once the deer emerged from behind the tree, I would have very little time to look at its antlers, decide to shoot and make the shot before it disappeared into the thick brush again.

It was the peak of the rut, and I knew how big the bucks of Gregory County, S.D., grew. I didn't want to fill my deer tag with anything less than a mature buck.

This was the third consecutive year I'd hunted at the Krieger Cattle Company of Burke, S.D., owned by Ken Krieger, a whitetail fanatic whose knowledge of game in the area is surpassed only by his hospitality and dedication to hunting.

In the two preceding years, I'd been fortunate enough to shoot what were at the time my two biggest bucks. I'd also become well-acquainted with the tremendous trophy potential of the whitetails inhabiting the hills and canyons of south-central South Dakota. After a lifetime of hunting in the East, the number of mature bucks I saw while hunting out West amazed me. I was even more impressed by the incredibly large bodies of South Dakota whitetails.

With this in mind, I impatiently waited for the deer to emerge from behind the tree and expose its head. As I watched, the deer rubbed its hind legs together and urinated over its hocks.

The deer finally stepped forward, revealing a set of massive, multitined antlers. I quickly centered the cross hairs behind the buck's shoulder and squeezed the trigger. As the rifle's report faded, I heard the solid thump of the bullet hitting the buck. The large-bodied buck collapsed in its tracks and lay motionless.

After watching the buck for a few minutes, I descended from my box stand and hiked across the ravine. I stood over the buck, awed by its huge body. I'd once shot a buck that weighed about 215 pounds on the hoof, but the one lying before me now was far larger.

After my shock at the deer's body size subsided, I turned my attention to the buck's heavy antlers.

The rack sported 10 points, including a long, nontypical dagger-like tine growing from the right base. The right main beam and its third point had been partially broken off and were about three inches shorter than those on the opposite side. Although the abnormal and broken points give the rack character, the rack's most impressive trait was its mass. I couldn't make contact between my fingers and thumb while reaching around the bases.

After hiking out from the stand, my guide and I returned with an all-terrain vehicle to haul out the deer. It took all of our combined strength to position the buck for photos.

After field dressing the deer, it was still so heavy we were barely able to load it onto the ATV. When we put the buck on the scales the next day, it weighed 200 pounds. Its live weight was probably more than 250 pounds.

Although I've been fortunate enough to shoot some fine deer, the body size and antler mass of this buck make it my most memorable deer. I am well aware, however, that even larger deer roam the hills and canyons of Burke, S.D.

You can bet that I'll be back looking for an even bigger buck this November.

— Mike Caldarelli

First Big Buck Sports Deformed Rack

Scott Newman of Waupun, Wis., usually gun-hunts the big woods of northern Wisconsin, near Michigan's Upper Peninsula. Although the area occasionally produces some big bucks, deer densities are low and action is often slow. Not surprisingly, Newman has faced an uphill battle for bagging mature bucks.

He hoped his luck would change during Wisconsin's 2002 firearms season, as he headed to central Wisconsin's Waupaca County to hunt the property of a family friend, Harvey Schaub.

HUNTER: **Scott Newman**
DATE: **November 2002**
LOCATION: **Waupaca Co., Wisconsin**
METHOD: **Shotgun**
RACK: **11-point buck**

Although he hadn't planned to hunt the afternoon he reached the property, Newman arrived with plenty of time to head to his stand for an evening hunt. His change of plans was about to pay-off.

About a half-hour before the end of shooting hours, Newman spotted a deer moving across the oak-covered ridge near his tower stand. At first, Newman thought it was a smaller buck, but then the deer turned it's head, revealing a wide, nontypical rack.

Excited by the chance at killing his first mature buck, Newman raised his shotgun and rested it against the rail of his stand. Despite his high hopes, Newman knew killing the deer wouldn't be a simple proposition. The buck was angling away from him, walking steadily at about 150 yards.

Newman steadied his rifled shotgun barrel on the shooting rail, centered the buck in his sights and squeezed the trigger.

At the shot, the buck flinched and trotted along the ridge, finally crashing against a tree.

After the shock wore off, Newman descended from his stand and rushed over to the buck. Although he knew the buck's rack was unusual, he had no idea how strange it really was.

The rack featured a normal 4-point left beam and a bizarre 7-point right beam that snaked almost perpendicular to the buck's head. The reason for the weird antler was immediately apparent: the buck was missing the bottom 9 inches of its left hind leg.

According to Newman, the buck was walking normally before he shot it, despite the handicap.

— RYAN GILLIGAN

Big 9-Pointer Earns Spot on the Wall

HUNTER: **Jeff Carpenter**
DATE: **November 2002**
LOCATION: **Missouri**
METHOD: **Rifle**
RACK: **9-point buck**

Jeff Carpenter of Gladstone, Mo., will never forget Missouri's 2002 gun season. From frantic deer activity to monster bucks, the season had it all.

On opening day, Carpenter hunted from his permanent stand on 40 acres of chest-high switch grass mixed with forests. The morning was action-packed. Deer were running everywhere. Bucks were rutting heavily, but Carpenter just couldn't get a shot at a buck during the frantic action. Carpenter tried grunting, but the bucks either ignored his calls or couldn't hear them above the frantic crashing through the switch grass.

Carpenter decided he needed a new plan for his second-day hunt. He put out some salt 20 yards from his stand, hoping to draw in some deer.

Day 2 was the complete opposite of opening day's action. The place was calm. By 7 a.m., Carpenter hadn't seen a deer!

Carpenter decided to create his own action, and blew on his grunt call. Motion caught his attention 40 yards away as a deer stood up behind a tree. Carpenter saw the buck's antlers protruding from either side of the tree, and he said it looked like a bush had just stood up from within the switch grass!

The buck approached, and when it was 30 yards away, Carpenter fired his rifle and the buck went down. Carpenter trembled uncontrollably with excitement. This buck was the biggest he'd seen in seven years of hunting the property. He saw the buck on opening day, but didn't get a shot at it.

When he'd settled down, Carpenter climbed out of his stand and walked to where the buck had stood. Carpenter's heart sank when he found no blood. Fortunately, his melancholy was short-lived, as he soon discovered a heavy blood trail. Carpenter found his big 9-pointer after trailing the deer for about 100 yards.

But now he faced a dilemma. Carpenter had always vowed his first head mount would be a 10-pointer, but his 9-pointer certainly was nice, and by far his biggest buck.

His hesitation was short-lived. After taking the deer home and snapping some photos, Carpenter called his taxidermist and told him that he would be stopping in shortly!

10-Pointer is Missouri Bow-Hunter's Biggest

Larry Williams of Holts Summit, Mo., will not soon forget Nov. 2, 2002.

That day Williams was hunting the woods of Callaway County, Missouri when he saw a 4-point buck licking a cedar tree just past his 30-yard marker.

While he watched the buck, motion to his left caught his eye. There, about 60 yards away, was a huge-bodied deer. When Williams saw the buck's antlers, he silently pleaded for the buck to come his way.

HUNTER: **Larry Williams**
DATE: **Nov. 2, 2002**
LOCATION: **Callaway Co., Missouri**
METHOD: **Bow**
RACK: **10-point buck**

Luck was with him that day, and the buck drew closer. Eventually, the big 10-pointer headed for the same licking branch the 4-pointer was working.

Although the 10-pointer was bigger than any buck Williams had ever shot, Williams remained calm. He drew his bow, reminded himself of the distance, and released his arrow.

Williams couldn't see the arrow's flight, but heard a thud. The buck took one bound and disappeared in the woods.

The excitement set in when the buck vanished. Williams' knees began shaking.

Williams waited as long as he could stand it, then proceeded to the cedar tree.

When he reached the tree, he saw no sign of a hit. Crazy thoughts ran through his head: Had he hit a tree or the ground instead of the buck?

He went another 10 feet and was relieved when found a good blood trail. After following the trail for about 35 yards down a hill, he found his dead 10-pointer!

The buck was Williams' biggest, but its size presented him with a challenge. Williams couldn't move the deer!

After a few failed attempts, Williams left the buck in the woods and went to get his friend Lawrence Redel. Even with Redel's help, the pair could not lift the buck onto their four-wheeler.

Finally, using a rope hoist, they managed to load the buck, which field dressed at 195 pounds.

Williams said he has bow-hunted for many years, but tagging this buck was his most exciting experience.

Bow-Hunter Rattles In His Best Buck

Bob Ogurcak, of York, Pa., hunted hard during the 2002 rut.

Ogurcak hunted for several consecutive days in mid-November, but didn't see much deer activity, due to warm weather. However, action picked up as a cold front approached.

On Nov. 15, Ogurcak saw plenty of deer on his morning hunt, including several bucks chasing does, but he couldn't get a shot. He left the woods optimistic for his afternoon hunt.

At 2 p.m., Ogurcak returned to the same stand. He thought he might get a shot that evening because the approaching storm would bring wet, windy weather. After settling down, he worked his rattling antlers, but nothing appeared.

HUNTER: **Bob Ogurcak**
DATE: **Nov. 15, 2002**
LOCATION: **Pennsylvania**
METHOD: **Bow**
RACK: **10-point buck 130-class**

Ogurcak rattled again about an hour later. This time he immediately heard crisp leaves rustling in a thicket about 100 yards to his left.

Ogurcak quickly hung up his antlers and turned to see a pair of white antlers bobbing toward him.

As the buck approached, it circled Ogurcak's tree and walked across a small knob and straight toward Ogurcak. When the buck was 30 yards away, Ogurcak drew, but the buck was coming straight on and presented no shot.

The buck kept advancing. Finally, when it was 8 yards away, it saw Ogurcak move, and it stopped. Ogurcak shot, and though at first he thought it was a bit high, he knew the severe angle would penetrate for a quick kill.

Ogurcak watched the buck run about 50 yards into the thicket, then all was quiet.

Ogurcak was certain he'd find his buck where he'd last seen it, but nonetheless sat on his stand until well after nightfall.

Ogurcak met a few friends back at his truck, then returned to search for the buck. It was laying exactly where he thought it would be.

The 10-pointer field dressed at more than 200 pounds, and the rack grossed 137 3/8 inches.

Hunter Tags Best Buck Despite Oversleeping

Every hunter has probably awoken in a panic suddenly in the middle of the night. We turn over and look at the clock and realize we didn't really oversleep for the big hunt — it was just a nightmare.

That nightmare became a reality for Doug Riste of Wausau, Wis., during the 2002 Wisconsin gun-hunting season.

Riste was supposed to meet his friend for a deer drive at 8 a.m. on the last morning of deer season, but he overslept.

Although he was late, he hurriedly dressed and arrived a half-hour late. Riste's friend had gone into town for breakfast, but Riste grabbed his rifle and headed for his friend's tree stand anyway.

HUNTER: **Doug Riste**
DATE: **Dec. 1, 2002**
LOCATION: **Wisconsin**
METHOD: **Rifle**
RACK: **8-point buck**

Riste reached the stand, but before he started his ascent up the ladder, he saw a deer coming out of the cedars. Riste raised his rifle and discovered the deer was a mature buck.

Riste scoped the buck and fired, but missed. He couldn't believe it. Thinking that he shot high, he held lower on his target and shot again, connecting with the buck's vitals.

Riste quickly covered the 75 yards between him and the buck and searched for blood.

Riste found the blood trail and had followed it for about 25 steps when he saw the buck laying down, looking at him. Riste held on the buck's shoulder (making sure not to hit the neck because he planned on getting a head mount) and shot again, killing the buck.

Riste's 2002 buck was the first 8-pointer he's killed in 35 years of hunting, although he has killed four half-rack 4-pointers. The buck had a 14¾-inch spread and 10-inch tines and field dressed at 180 pounds.

Riste had seen the buck about 30 yards from where he shot him in August.

Riste said sometimes it pays to sleep in before donning hunting clothes for the last hunt of the season!

Prepared Bow-Hunter Connects on New Shot

Eric Sprigler of New Albany, Ind., was prepared for the 2000 bow season. He had secured permission to hunt in several areas, and all that summer he glassed deer and hung his stands. So when bow season opened, he thought he was ready for anything.

On Oct. 3, Sprigler was hunting a farm near Floyds Knobs, Ind. He had seen a good-sized 8-pointer on this farm on several occasions.

HUNTER: **Eric Sprigler**
DATE: **Oct. 3, 2000**
LOCATION: **Indiana**
METHOD: **Bow**
RACK: **8-point buck**

Early that morning, Sprigler quietly climbed into his stand, 25 feet up a tree. The wind was perfect, and the day was just beginning to unfold.

Just as the sun was about to light up the morning, Sprigler saw a good buck leaving an alfalfa field and coming toward him. Sprigler had placed his stand in the buck's bedding area in a honeysuckle thicket, and his preseason scouting was about to pay off.

However, the buck walked past his stand at about 30 yards and didn't present Sprigler with a shot. The buck disappeared into the thicket.

Sprigler thought the buck was gone, but 5 minutes later, he caught movement on his left. It was the buck, and it was coming right toward him!

Sprigler drew his bow, and the buck walked to within 1 foot of the tree Sprigler was in! It even licked the bark of Sprigler's tree. Amazingly, the buck had no idea Sprigler was directly above.

Now came the moment of truth. Despite all of Sprigler's preseason scouting trips and overall preparations, he had never attempted a straight-down shot. He decided today was the day to give the shot a try.

Sprigler placed his sight pin about half way back on the buck and released.

The arrow penetrated the left lung and exited through the deer's belly. The buck collapsed after running 40 yards.

Sprigler's 8-pointer field dressed at 185 pounds and is his biggest to date, but he said he's confident he can shoot a larger buck in the future.

Best Buck Appears On Mid-Morning Bow-Hunt

Most bow-hunters rise early to take advantage of early morning deer activity. But on Nov. 2, 2001, Chip Miller of Cudahy, Wis., slept in.

But it wasn't an oversight on Miller's part.

Miller has seen several mature bucks where he hunts in central Wisconsin, and he frequently sees the big boys cruising from 9 a.m. to noon.

Miller scaled a tree with his climbing tree stand later in the morning to take advantage of the area's mid-morning big-buck movement. The weather was clear and sunny — not classic big-buck weather — but that didn't slow down buck movement.

HUNTER: **Chip Miller**
DATE: **Nov. 2, 2001**
LOCATION: **Wisconsin**
METHOD: **Bow**
RACK: **8-point buck**

Miller rattled and grunted every half-hour, and had just finished one of these calling sequences around 10:30 a.m. when an 8-pointer came down the ridge to investigate.

The buck walked toward Miller, approaching to well within bow range.

Miller waited until the buck's eyes were behind a tree before drawing his bow.

The tall-racked 8-pointer was quartering away at 13 yards when Miller aimed, then launched his arrow.

Miller thought his shot was perfect when he released, but the buck simply strolled off and showed no visible signs of being hit.

When he saw the buck's reaction, Miller questioned his shot.

The deer walked along a ridge for 120 yards, and Miller saw it bed.

The more he thought about his shot, Miller reasoned that no two deer react the same way to arrow wounds. Miller was sure he had been on target, and he remained optimistic.

Just to be safe, Miller quietly slipped out of the area and didn't return to follow his deer until after dark. When he did, he found the buck dead in the bed where he'd watched it lie down hours earlier.

Miller's long-tined 8-pointer field dressed at 188 pounds.

Brian Lovett
Alabama, January 2003
9-pointer
Brian Lovett

Maryland Hunter Scores During Post-Rut Hunt

When most deer hunters think of trophy whitetails, Maryland probably isn't the first state that comes to mind. But when you live in Maryland, you have to hunt where you can, and that's exactly what Greg Dorworth of Gaithersburg, Md., does.

Dorworth is a die-hard bow-hunter who hunts every chance he gets. Despite his persistence, he's never had an opportunity to shoot what most people would classify as a trophy buck. Still, that doesn't deter him from his passion for deer hunting.

However, deer hunting — especially bow-hunting — success isn't measured by general consensus. Dorworth considers the 2001 bow season — when he shot his biggest buck yet — an overwhelming success. And he couldn't be more proud of the deer he shot.

HUNTER: **Greg Dorworth**
DATE: **Nov. 17, 2001**
LOCATION: **Montgomery Co., Maryland**
METHOD: **Bow**
RACK: **6-point buck**

Dorworth hunts in Montgomery County, Md. On Nov. 17, 2001, he reached his stand at about 2 p.m. on a clear, mild day. The rut was mostly over where Dorworth hunts, and deer had entered a post-rut pattern.

The first two hours on stand yielded no deer sightings, but at 4:15, Dorworth was startled by a loud commotion. A doe blasted out of a thicket, and judging by its actions, Dorworth expected a buck to follow.

He was right. A 6-point buck was right behind the doe. It lip-curled as it walked.

Dorworth drew his bow and waited for the buck to walk into a shooting lane. It did, but it didn't stop walking.

Dorworth whistled and the buck stopped broadside about 22 yards away. Before the buck located the source of the noise, Dorworth sent his arrow on its way.

Dorworth's shot was perfect, penetrating both lungs. The 6-pointer ran only 60 yards before succumbing to the hit.

Dorworth's 6-pointer dressed at 155 pounds.

Climbing Stand Helps Hunter Shoot Buck

John Lee of Grantsville, Md., takes a yearly trip to northeastern Missouri to hunt the Show-Me State's whitetails. In his three years of booking hunts in Missouri, he has done quite well, shooting three does and two bucks with his bow. But none of the deer compared to the one he shot Nov. 4, 2002.

That evening was the third of Lee's six-day hunt. It was cool and overcast, and Lee hoped there would be buck activity before dark. Lee had borrowed a new climbing tree stand from a friend and set up in a tree where his guide told him to sit.

HUNTER: **John Lee**
DATE: **Nov. 4, 2002**
LOCATION: **Missouri**
METHOD: **Bow**
RACK: **9-point buck**

Lee had good action, spotting three different bucks, one of which came to investigate his rattling sequence. However, Lee didn't shoot.

At about 4:45 p.m., following a heavy rattling sequence, Lee spotted a fourth buck. This one really grabbed his attention. It was the buck he had been waiting for.

The buck was battle-scarred and was seeking out the "fight" that it had heard. It offered Lee a 25-yard broadside shot, and Lee connected on the 9-pointer. Lee saw the buck fall after it ran 80 yards.

When Lee climbed down from his tree to recover his buck, he realized the aggressive deer had thrown caution to the wind without learning from its mistakes. Amazingly, Lee discovered the 9-pointer he'd killed was the same buck he'd rattled in the night before, but the first night he couldn't get a shot at it! Luckily for Lee, he'd gotten a second chance.

When caping the deer, it was obvious the buck had been in numerous fights. The buck looked "beat up" and bore many battle wounds.

Lee's 9-pointer field dressed at 200 pounds and is the largest buck he has ever shot with his bow.

Lee has already booked his next Missouri hunt in coordination with the rut.

Shooting your best buck on an out-of-state hunt is not a bad way to break in a new climbing tree stand, especially if it's not even yours!

Dead Duck Helps Hunter Bag 12-Point Buck

Bill Brundage of Bath, N.Y., couldn't have imagined that trying to retrieve a dead duck from his pond in September 2002 would help him shoot the biggest buck of his life in November, but sometimes strange circumstances lead to strange results.

Brundage stretched to reach the dead duck with a potato hook and strained a bit too far, causing him great pain.

HUNTER: **Bill Brundage**
DATE: **Nov. 21, 2002**
LOCATION: **New York**
METHOD: **Gun**
RACK: **12-point buck**

When deer season rolled around, Brundage's hunting partners told him he could post instead of walk during their deer drives because he was still ailing from the strain he put on his body two months earlier.

Brundage, a farmer, hunts with several neighboring farmers. They drive each others' land and then have a venison dinner after the season. The event draws 60 to 75 people!

On Nov. 21, Brundage led the standers to their posts at 11 a.m. The drivers were scheduled to come through at 1 p.m.

Brundage saw eight deer run past him, but they were too far away. He repositioned himself to prevent deer from going past him again. Minutes later, a driver shot, and two does ran past, still too far away.

Finally, a huge buck appeared 60 yards away. Brundage couldn't tear his eyes from the magic of the buck's wide rack. He was so enraptured with the buck's antlers he forgot to take the safety off before he pulled the trigger, and nothing happened when he tried to fire.

Now Brundage had to wait for the buck to clear some trees. Brundage was so excited, he doesn't remember aiming, but when he pulled the trigger, the buck dropped.

Brundage said he was fortunate to shoot the deer because he usually walks on deer drives. He also admitted that Lady Luck was with him that day.

Brundage's hunting partners insisted the 12-point buck, whose inside spread was more than 20 inches, should be head-mounted, and they even pitched in to help with the cost of getting it mounted.

What a great bunch of hunting pals!

Hunter Misses Photo Op But Bags Monster Buck

Jeff Tirri of Hubertus, Wis., is remodeling his recreation room in his basement. He has to in order to find space for the full-body mount of the 262-pound, 14-point buck he shot. (Yes, that's the dressed weight!)

Tirri hunts private land in Wisconsin's famous Buffalo County. In the early season, he likes to hunt between a bedding area and a clover field with a pond, and that's where he chose to sit Oct. 19, 2002.

HUNTER: **Jeff Tirri**
DATE: **Oct. 20, 2002**
LOCATION: **Buffalo Co., Wisconsin**
METHOD: **Bow**
RACK: **14-point buck, 170-class**

Before taking a stand that evening, Tirri decided to relocate his remote-sensing camera. He wanted to put it on a large pine tree 10 yards from a scrape, but ended up positioning it in another tree about 10 yards from the big pine instead.

After moving the camera, Tirri climbed into his stand. That evening Tirri saw a doe and a fawn come to the clover field, and behind them was a nice 9-pointer. However, Tirri didn't get a shot at the buck.

The following evening Tirri hunted from the same stand. Once again a doe and fawn entered the clover field, and Tirri hoped the big 9-pointer would reappear. Although he didn't see the 9-pointer again, Tirri wasn't disappointed.

Instead, at about 5:40, a huge buck emerged and trotted uphill toward the feeding deer. The buck was cruising down a trail would lead past Tirri's stand at only 8 yards.

Tirri hunts 25 feet up, so when the buck came past, it was at a severe angle. However, Tirri's shot broke the buck's spine and dropped it in its tracks.

When Tirri climbed down to look at the deer, he couldn't believe his eyes. The buck sported 14 points and a 20$^{5}/_{8}$-inch inside spread. The rack grossed 188$^{6}/_{8}$ inches and netted 173$^{7}/_{8}$ inches. The deer was 5$^{1}/_{2}$ years old, and Tirri's neighbor had found the buck's sheds from the last three seasons.

Tirri was obviously happy with his luck, but there was a downside. If he'd have positioned his remote-sensing camera on the big pine tree like he wanted to, he'd have snapped a picture of the bruiser buck moments before he killed it!

Randy Berwald
Missouri, November 1999
180-class 18-pointer

Southern Hunting Trip Produces Biggest Buck

Anthony Vaccarelli of Mahopac, N.Y., takes a hunting trip every year with his partner, Charlie. They have traveled to Wyoming and Canada to hunt whitetails, but decided to try something a little different in 2002.

Vaccarelli and Charlie met an outfitter from South Carolina at the Harrisburg, Pa., Outdoorsman's Show and were impressed by the description of his hunting operation. They booked a hunt.

HUNTER: **Anthony Vaccarelli**
DATE: **November 2002**
LOCATION: **South Carolina**
METHOD: **.270 Rifle**
RACK: **9-point buck, 130-class**

In November 2002, they traveled to South Carolina for their annual deer hunt. They were hoping to experience some warm weather instead of the cold they often encountered on their hunts at home and out of state. The only problem was, Vaccarelli thought that Southern whitetails carried small antlers. He had a lot to learn!

The first day of the hunt, Vaccarelli entered his tower stand overlooking a large food plot at 6 a.m. Charlie's stand was positioned about 400 yards from Vaccarelli's.

Every hour the two hunting partners radioed each other to learn of any deer sightings. Things were pretty slow. Charlie saw three does at 9:30, and Vaccarelli saw one at 10:30. They decided to meet on a logging road halfway between their stands at noon for lunch.

However, as mid-day neared, something told Vaccarelli that he should stay on stand a little longer. Instead of meeting Charlie at the logging road for lunch, Vaccarelli ate his lunch in his stand, then took a 20-minute nap in the warm, sunny, 55-degree weather.

It was a good thing Vaccarelli listened to his gut.

When he awoke at 12:30, he learned that his hunch to stay put was dead on. Vaccarelli saw a huge 9-pointer about 120 yards away.

Vaccarelli shouldered his .270, aimed carefully, and fired. The 9-pointer stumbled and fell.

The 130-class 9-pointer is Vaccarelli's best in 22 years of hunting. Vaccarelli is now a believer in the quality of Southern deer, and he intends to hunt in the South again soon.

Minnesota Monster Rejuvenates Spirit

Killing a trophy buck is an incredible accomplishment for anyone, but one Minnesota hunter overcame more than just the animal's keen survival instincts to kill hers.

Carrie Szczech Kott-Lampert of Chisago City, Minn., has hunted deer every year since 1983, except 1993. That year, she waited seven months for a heart transplant, and suffered the many pains associated with the life-saving, life-changing procedure.

HUNTER: **Carrie Szczech Kott-Lampert**
DATE: **November 2002**
LOCATION: **Minnesota**
METHOD: **.30-06 Rifle**
RACK: **14-point buck, 170-class**

Kott-Lampert didn't know if she would have a chance to hunt during the 2002 deer season. She and her husband sold their house and 20-acre farm about a month before deer season opened, which made life hectic.

The rigors of moving, combined with her everyday problems after her heart transplant, made her weak and ill. For example, Kott-Lampert describes the aftermath of a heart transplant as being like a chronic illness that never heals. She is severely hearing impaired, often has blurred vision and frequently uses a cane or wheelchair to help her get around.

Still, she is thankful for each day. She and her husband try to procure their own meat as much as possible, and when the person who bought the house from them asked if they wanted to hunt on their old property, she decided to hunt after all.

Nov. 9 was a warm Saturday, and, as usual, Kott-Lampert decided to hunt all day if necessary.

About 10:00, some neighbors shot a deer and dragged it to a power line right of way within sight of Kott-Lampert's stand. Several people assembled around the deer, and Kott-Lampert grew aggravated by their boisterous activity. The noise certainly wasn't helping her chances of sighting a deer.

Finally the hunters went back to their cabin for lunch, and things settled down.

At about 11:45, Kott-Lampert heard them returning. She scanned the field in front of her intently, hoping the noisy hunters would jump a deer from its bed and send it her way.

Her eyes swiveled from side to side, and finally she did a double take when she noticed a huge brown object that wasn't there before.

She realized it was a big deer, and it had a rack. The buck was prancing through a field of golden grass, and that image is forever burned into her mind. She said seeing the buck in the field was like seeing the ocean for the first time.

Alhough she would have liked to have watched the buck a little longer, there was no time to wait if she wanted to take her once-in-a-lifetime shot.

Kott-Lampert quickly shouldered her .30-06 and fired. The buck dropped. She fired a follow-up shot to finish the mortally wounded buck.

Kott-Lampert shed a couple tears over the buck's death and said a quick prayer as things sunk in.

Kott-Lampert is no stranger to big bucks. In fact, she shot a big 10-pointer on her very first deer hunt. But the buck that lay dead in the field was much bigger than any buck she had ever seen before.

She waited five minutes to make sure the buck was down for good, then whistled for her husband, who was sitting about 500 yards away.

As he made his way toward his wife, he saw the monster whitetail laying in the field and started walking to it, but Kott-Lampert waved him back over to her stand. She wanted to be the first to see her tremendous buck up close!

When she finally got a good look at the buck, she was in disbelief. Never before had she seen a buck that compared to this one. The monster buck carried 14 points with a 23½-inch inside spread. The rack green scored 171⅞ inches, and field dressed at 208 pounds.

When she brought the deer to town to register it, a crowd of about 30 people gathered around her to shake her hand or give her a hug.

But for Kott-Lampert, the buck is more than just a trophy to hang on the wall.

At the time, Kott-Lampert had been feeling sick, and was coping with the loss of much of her hair. The beautiful image of the buck in the field and the excitement of shooting it raised her spirits at a time when they were very low. She views the buck as a gift from God.

Kott-Lampert's taxidermist is creating a half-body mount of her exceptional buck, and already people are stopping in, impatiently waiting to see it.

Hunter Sneaks Up Hill, Finds 18-Pointer

Dec. 5, 2002 — the first day of Illinois' second 2002 shotgun season — was bitterly cold and snowy. However, it's a day Mike Robards of Homer, Ill., will not soon forget.

Robards spent opening day hunting on a friend's Clark County farm.

Two inches of snow had fallen the night before, and the temperature was only 5 degrees for the morning hunt. But the bitterly cold December weather didn't deter Robards from his plan. He hoped to find an active mature buck roaming the frigid Illinois landscape.

HUNTER: **Mike Robards**
DATE: **Dec. 5, 2002**
LOCATION: **Clark Co., Illinois**
METHOD: **Shotgun**
RACK: **18-point buck, 180-class**

In the morning, Robards hunted in a deep draw with a cut soybean field on the ridge above it. He only saw one small buck, which he passed up.

For his afternoon hunt, Robards decided to set up where he'd seen the small buck earlier that morning.

By 4 p.m., he'd seen only a pair of does, so Robards left his post in the draw and decided to sneak up the side of the draw to take a peek at the picked soybean field. He hoped deer might come out to feed early because of the miserable weather.

When he peered over the top of the draw, he saw a large-bodied deer with its head down just 50 yards away. Robards shouldered his shotgun and scoped the big deer.

When the deer raised its head, Robards saw that it was a buck with an enormous rack, and Robards immediately knew this was the buck he'd been waiting for.

However, before Robards could shoot, the buck bolted. In his haste to shoot, Robards missed the deer on his first shot, but but his slug connected with the fleeing whitetail on his second attempt.

Robards' large-bodied 18-point buck gross scored about 180 inches and field dressed at 200 pounds.

Amazingly, no one in Robards' hunting party had ever seen the heavy-racked 18-point buck previously.

Hunter's 50th Deer Is One For the Wall

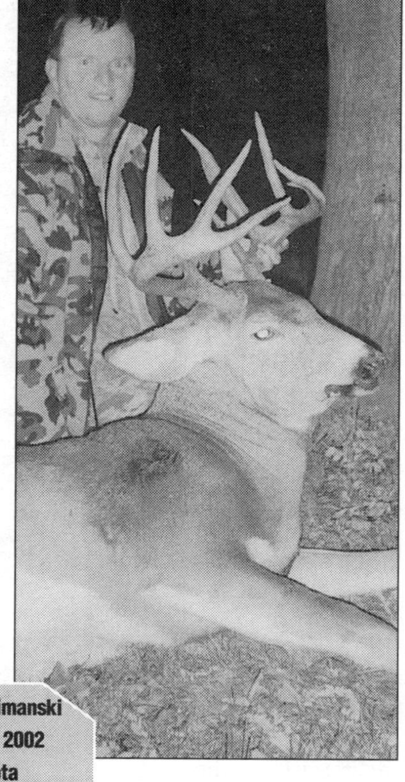

Shelly Simanski of Red Wing, Minn., has hunted for 32 years. In that time, he has shot a lot of bucks and does and had the racks from some of his larger bucks mounted, but he'd never shot one that he believed was worthy of a head mount. At least not until Minnesota's 2002 gun-deer season.

During the early bow season, Simanski shot a doe and passed up four small bucks. When shotgun season opened, he decided he would only shoot a buck that was at least 2½ years old.

Early in the season, Simanski saw the same four bucks he'd seen during bow season, but he stuck to his plan of holding out for a bigger buck.

HUNTER: **Shelly Simanski**
DATE: **Nov. 21, 2002**
LOCATION: **Minnesota**
METHOD: **Shotgun**
RACK: **10-point buck, 150-class**

On Nov. 21, he took off work an hour early and was in his tree stand by 2:15 p.m. However, the early start didn't help him because by 4 p.m., he still hadn't seen a deer.

Simanski decided to try to create some deer activity, and used a bleat can to produce three loud bleats. He'd hardly finished the third bleat when a large-bodied buck appeared about 80 yards away.

The buck was heading toward Simanski, apparently drawn by the bleats. It didn't take Simanski long to decide to shoot.

When the buck was 50 yards away, it turned broadside and looked in Simanski's direction. Simanski shouldered his shotgun, found the buck's front shoulder in his 2X scope and fired.

The big buck jumped and took off. Simanski was sure of his shot and didn't shoot again. The buck piled up after running about 60 yards.

The 10-pointer was the 50th deer Simanski has killed. The rack measured 157⅞ typical inches. Simanski is pleased that he finally shot a buck large enough for a head mount.

South Carolina Man Shoots Best Doe

Dan Hess and his daughter, Amanda, of Greer, S.C., went hunting Nov. 9, 2002. Little did they know, this hunt would be unlike any hunt they'd ever experienced.

Dan was disappointed that the wind was blowing out of the north, but Amanda remained optimistic as she climbed into her tower stand.

After seeing his daughter was safely in her stand, Dan continued on to the ground blind that he and Amanda had constructed the previous day.

Dan's stand bordered a clay road that meandered through a pine plantation near a stream. There were several heavy deer trails in the area, but the north wind would make hunting difficult.

HUNTER: **Dan Hess**
DATE: **Nov. 9, 2002**
LOCATION: **South Carolina**
METHOD: **.30-06 Rifle**
RACK: **8-point doe**

For the next two hours, Dan mostly observed the trails to the north, reasoning there was a better chance deer upwind of him would not smell him. However, he occasionally glanced over his shoulder, looking at the trails to the south.

Around 8:30 a.m., Dan was surprised to see a deer standing in the road 30 yards downwind. The deer had a large rack for its body size, and it appeared to have multiple drop tines and kicker points.

The deer stared at the blind, sensing something wasn't right.

His movements shielded by the blind, Dan shouldered his .30-06 and shot. The deer dropped in its tracks.

Amanda heard the shot and joined her father to see his deer. She commented on the deer's small hoofs and the fact that its antlers were still covered with velvet.

It wasn't until they took their deer to a meat locker that they discovered the deer was actually a doe!

The doe sported 8 points and had a 17-inch inside spread. The "drop tines and kicker points" were merely strips of peeling velvet.

Hunter Sees Few Deer, But the Wait Pays Off

HUNTER: **Scott Walck**
DATE: **Nov. 19, 2002**
LOCATION: **Maine**
METHOD: **Gun**
RACK: **15-point buck**

Although Scott Walck's annual Maine deer hunting trip is always memorable, he had a little more to celebrate after his 2002 hunt.

Walck, along with his son, Jeremiah, and friends Larry Albert and Armand Laub, made their 16th annual trip to the Big Woods of Maine.

Walck spent the first day scouting the area. First he went to his ace-in-the-hole spot where he finds scrapes every year. Sure enough, the place was littered with them. After poking around in other areas, he decided his best bet was to stick with the first spot.

On Day 2, Walck returned to set up his stand. When he was satisfied with his setup, he climbed into the stand and waited. A short time later he heard leaves rustling, then he heard a deer snort. After spooking the deer, Walck didn't see another deer all day.

On Day 3, Walck could see no deer had visited the area during the night. He hunted elsewhere but saw nothing.

Day 4 brought 10 inches of snow, and Walck spent the entire day scouting. Again, he didn't find any areas more promising than his original site, so he planned to return Monday morning.

On Monday there was a large set of tracks leading to the scrape. Walck hunted there all day, but saw no deer.

Tuesday was the day. That morning there was a dusting of snow, and two sets of tracks led to the scrape.

Walck climbed into his stand at about 7 a.m., and 45 minutes later he heard a noise behind him. When he turned, he saw movement. Unfortunately, because of his awkward position, he knew he would only be able to attempt a left-handed shot.

When the deer was 40 yards away, Walck saw antlers and shot. The buck ran 10 yards closer, and Walck saw it had a bigger rack than he'd expected. He shot again and the 15-point monarch dropped.

Father and Son Bag Best Bucks in 2002

The 2002 hunting season will always be memorable for the Wright family of Franklin, N.J. Greg shot his largest buck ever, and his son, John, shot his first buck.

Greg scored first. In mid-November, he traveled to Saskatchewan for a hunt he had booked on the Cree Reservation two years earlier.

The open fields with heavy thickets were much different than his hunting area in New Jersey, but they were excellent whitetail habitat.

The plan was to hunt from a blind his guide prepared and sit from dawn until dusk. The temperature was 19 degrees below zero.

HUNTER: **Greg Wright**
DATE: **November 2002**
LOCATION: **Saskatchewan**
METHOD: **Gun**
RACK: **12-point buck**

At daybreak, Greg saw two does and a 6-point buck. The young buck was the largest deer he'd ever seen, but not the deer he'd traveled 2,000 miles to shoot.

At 9:30, Greg saw a nice 8-pointer, but again it wasn't a shooter.

Another hour passed, and two bucks appeared, sizing up each other, hair bristled and ears laid back. Greg watched intently as the bucks locked antlers briefly before the larger buck chased the smaller one away.

Around 11:30, movement caught Greg's eye. Two does nervously walked into the open, watching their back trails in the thick Canadian bush. Greg raised his rifle just in case. Fifteen minutes later, a 12-pointer with split brow tines emerged from the alders. It was the buck he was looking for!

Greg scoped the 12-pointer, standing 110 yards away, aimed and fired. The buck kicked its hind legs, and Greg knew it wasn't going far. The buck raced only about 50 yards before dropping.

Greg's 12-point buck field dressed at 250 pounds and ranks as the largest buck he has killed in many years of deer hunting.

Ten days later it was John's turn.

He hoped to tag his first buck during New Jersey's special youth hunt.

Greg and John packed enough lunch and snacks for a day in the ground blind that Greg had built a few days earlier on the family farm.

At about 7:30, two does ambled past the stand at about 35 yards, but John was hoping for a chance at a buck, so he let the does walk.

Father and son had a good time whispering back and forth and enjoying the hunt, but when 10 a.m. arrived without another deer sighting, they decided to still-hunt a ridge with a thick cedar thicket.

Keeping the wind in their faces, Greg and John climbed the back side of the ridge without making too much noise. As they crested the ridge, the wind swirled slightly and carried their scent into the bedding area. Deer popped up everywhere! At least 10 deer ran to the left, with more headed downhill. John picked out a buck in the herd that went to the left.

The herd stopped 70 yards away, and John shifted about 10 feet until he had a clear shot at the standing buck. Greg knelt down and held out his arm to help steady John's shotgun.

When John shot, the buck whirled around before crashing downhill.

When John and Greg got to where the buck had stood, they found a massive blood trail leading into the cedars. The buck hadn't gone far. They found it piled up next to a blowdown 25 yards down the slope.

John excitedly rushed to his first buck, very proud of his 5-pointer. He looked up at Greg and said shooting the buck was the most exciting thing he'd ever done in his life.

Greg was just as proud of his son, and happy that they were able to share the moment together.

A best buck and a first buck in the same season — who could ask for more?

HUNTER: **John Wright**
DATE: **November 2002**
LOCATION: **New Jersey**
METHOD: **Shotgun**
RACK: **5-point buck**

Hunter Experiences Dream Deer Season

HUNTER: **Paul Kovach**
DATE: **Nov. 8, 2002**
LOCATION: **Minnesota**
METHOD: **Bow**
RACK: **10-point buck**

Minnesota's 2002 archery season started off well for Paul Kovach of Duluth, Minn. He saw more big bucks during bow-season than he had in 20-plus years of hunting.

Kovach spotted a nice buck a week before rifle season opened, and on Nov. 8, the day before rifle season, he figured it would be his last chance to see the buck.

By 9 a.m., Kovach had seen several small bucks and some does, but something didn't feel quite right. He trusted his instincts and moved to a new stand.

The new stand immediately felt right. After waiting a few minutes for things to settle down, Kovach rattled and grunted. Several minutes later, he heard a heavy thud upwind of him.

Beyond the tree he had just moved from was a large-bodied deer. When it moved, Kovach saw it was a nice buck. It was even bigger than the one he'd spotted earlier that week.

The buck moved closer, but when it didn't see any bucks fighting, it retreated.

Kovach grunted and tickled his antlers together, but the buck paid him no heed. In desperation, Kovach bleated and the buck stopped and looked back. Kovach bleated again and the buck started coming in from more than 100 yards away.

Each time the buck looked away, Kovach bleated. When the buck was 40 yards away, Kovach stopped calling for fear of spooking his prey.

The buck hung up and again turned to leave, but Kovach kept things going with another bleat. The buck approached more aggressively this time.

Kovach drew, but when the buck stopped, it was facing him head-on. It was all Kovach could do to hold the bow at full draw as his arms burned and shook. Finally, the buck turned. Kovach let the bow down, and the arrow jumped off the rest.

The buck was headed for an opening about 25 yards away where Kovach would have one last shot at it if he could draw his bow.

Using all his strength, Kovach brought the bow to full draw and watched his arrow sail in slow motion before it penetrated the buck's chest.

Kovach found no blood or hair, but zigzagged until he spotted his fallen buck.

The 10-pointer was his biggest ever, but things were about to get even better.

Later that season, Kovach headed to Manitoba for his first Canadian deer hunt.

As he traveled, he spotted five huge bucks within a 30-mile stretch, and his excitement level soared.

But Canadian deer don't come easy, he learned, after seeing only a spike buck the first day.

HUNTER: **Paul Kovach**
DATE: **2002**
LOCATION: **Manitoba**
METHOD: **Gun**
RACK: **10-point buck**

By Day 3, Kovach had only seen one nice buck, but it had broken points. Kovach decided to hold out for a bigger deer.

Hunting continued to test Kovach's patience, as few deer sightings combined with pouring rain, freezing rain and subzero temperatures.

By the end of the first week, Kovach was frustrated.

He called his wife and voiced his frustration. Her encouragement, along with his guide's offer to stay as long as he liked, renewed his enthusiasm for the hunt.

He decided to hunt for two more days.

Kovach was stationed in a new area for the next day, and as he walked to his stand that morning, he had a feeling it would be his day.

In mid-morning, Kovach saw a doe, and decided to move closer to where it traveled in hopes that a nice buck would follow.

Fatigue set in from hunting hard for eight days, and Kovach began to nod off, but he snapped alert because he felt something was approaching.

Sure enough, a high-tined buck emerged from the thick Canadian bush 60 yards away.

Kovach quickly sized up the buck and shot. The buck went down after a 30-yard scramble, and Kovach scurried to his second 10-pointer of his exciting 2002 season.

No. 7 Proves Hunter's Lucky Number

John Woods Jr. of Rossiter, Pa., was hunting with his brother and father 20 miles from home on the second day of Pennsylvania's deer season.

Around lunchtime, Woods' father decided to go home because he had some errands to run. The younger Woods didn't want to stop hunting, so when they got home, he went in the woods behind their house.

HUNTER: **John Woods Jr.**
DATE: **1988**
LOCATION: **Pennsylvania**
METHOD: **Gun**
RACK: **9-point buck**

Woods had barely entered the forest when he spotted a deer about 150 yards away. However, the cover was too thick to determine if it was a buck or a doe, and Woods stared at the deer for about 10 minutes before he spotted the buck's antlers.

The cover was pretty thick, and Woods watched the deer feed for 10 minutes before trying a shot at the buck.

When Woods finally shot, he missed. To his surprise, the buck stayed where it was for a moment before running straight at the hunter.

Woods shot again but saw the bark fly off a pine tree.

The buck still had no idea where the shooting was coming from and continued its flight toward Woods.

Woods kept shooting at the buck, but he only hit trees, due to the thick growth. Finally, he realized he'd unloaded all six cartridges without touching the buck.

Normally, Woods doesn't carry extra bullets with him, and he frantically searched his pockets for more ammunition.

Amazingly he found a seventh shell deep in his pocket. He loaded it and vowed to make it count if he got the chance. However, the buck was gone.

Woods walked to where he'd last seen the buck. He couldn't find any blood in the numerous tracks in the area. Finally, Woods just walked where he thought the buck was headed, and there was the buck, bedded down 40 yards away. The buck was panting and looking the other direction, presumably trying to find the hunter.

Woods made good on his seventh shot, and by the time his father got home from running errands, the buck was hanging on the front porch and Woods was finally eating his lunch.

Shift Change at Work Doesn't Stop Hunter

Maybe it was sheer determination, dumb luck or destiny, but Bob Keller of Vesper, Wis., shot his biggest buck ever on the third day of Wisconsin's 2002 gun-deer season.

Keller had just changed shifts at work, which fouled up his hunting plans. Nevertheless, on the third day of season (a Monday) Keller left work at about 2:30 with the intention of getting in a quick afternoon hunt.

HUNTER: **Bob Keller**
DATE: **Nov. 25, 2002**
LOCATION: **Wisconsin**
METHOD: **.30-06 Rifle**
RACK: **13-point buck**

Keller reached his stand about 3:30, and had only been sitting for about 10 minutes when he heard a deer walking behind him.

Keller turned to look and saw a nice rack sticking up out of the brush.

Though Keller was 20 feet up a tree, the buck apparently saw him turn, and walked off into the brush.

Keller could still see the deer, so he watched it for about five minutes. However, the cover was too thick to permit a shot.

Keller thought that he simply wouldn't get a shot at the huge buck, but then he realized that the deer was moving toward a long shooting lane that he'd cut through the brush.

When the buck popped into the lane 60 yards away, Keller shouldered his .30-06 and fired.

The buck didn't react at all. It merely ran off.

Keller heard the buck go over the top of a hill, and heard the telltale sound of a deer crashing. He knew his shot was true.

Keller climbed down from his stand and found a heavy blood trail. When he first saw the buck, its head was straight up. Keller almost shot again, but realized the buck was dead and its massive rack was holding it aloft.

Keller's buck sported 13 points and an 18½-inch inside spread. Perhaps the most impressive feature was the rack's basal circumference: a whopping 8½ inches.

Keller said bucks in his area often have nice racks, but they're not known for their mass.

Many of Keller's friends went "up North" for deer season, but Keller bagged his trophy close to home.

Hunter Finds His Buck After Worrisome Night

Elmer Jantzi of Central Square, N.Y., experienced a roller coaster of emotions on his Nov. 12, 2001 hunt.

Previous experience had taught him not to hunt a breeding area where he hunted before that day, so when the date finally arrived, he anxiously entered the breeding area, optimistic about his chances to shoot a nice buck as the rut kicked in.

In the morning, he went to his observation stand to scope out deer activity, and then moved to his primary stand around 9 a.m. However, two dogs appeared and wouldn't stop barking. Jantzi had to climb down from his stand to shoo the dogs away, and his hunt was ruined.

HUNTER: **Elmer Jantzi**
DATE: **Nov. 12, 2001**
LOCATION: **New York**
METHOD: **Bow**
RACK: **10-point buck, 120-class**

Jantzi returned to his primary stand that afternoon, hoping things had settled down after the morning's clamoring.

He saw a small 6-pointer at 3:30 p.m. About 15 minutes later, he made a tending grunt, hoping to pull a big boy out of a nearby apple orchard.

Jantzi's calling worked. A nice 10-pointer appeared 25 yards away. Jantzi was shocked by the buck's body size and massive antlers.

The buck stood broadside 25 yards away. Before Jantzi could get into position for a shot, the buck lowered its head to pick up an apple, and then stood with its head up, staring at Jantzi. Luckily it didn't see the concealed hunter, who was perched in a multiple-trunked maple only 12 feet up.

When the buck finished the fruit, it turned and walked toward another shooting lane.

Jantzi shuffled his feet when the buck was behind a blown-down apple tree, but couldn't draw in time. He resisted the temptation to draw when the buck was in the open, and waited until a black cherry tree screened his movements.

His bow never felt so heavy and awkward in his hands, even though he'd been hunting with it for 13 years. Although he'd been watching the buck for 15 minutes, when the moment came to draw his bow, he didn't feel ready. However, he had to hurry as the buck quickly cleared the cherry tree.

Jantzi managed to draw the bow, and when the buck entered the shooting lane, he centered his 20-yard sight pin and released his arrow.

Jantzi heard the arrow hit the deer and saw the fletching protruding from just behind the buck's shoulder as it dashed back into the orchard with its head up and tail down.

When the buck disappeared, Jantzi could finally breathe again, and a big smile spread across his face.

Pulling himself together to shoot the buck was the most difficult hunting situation he'd ever been in, but he'd done it. He thought he'd soon recover the buck.

When he climbed down from his tree stand, however, he couldn't find blood or his arrow. He searched for a while, and then decided to postpone the search till morning.

The night was a restless one for Jantzi. He began questioning himself, even though he'd seen the fletchings in the deer. His thoughts ranged from giving up hunting to recovering the buck. In the end, he decided no one knew the area better than he did, and he was determined to track down his deer.

The following morning Jantzi awoke to an inch of new-fallen snow. He didn't know if the fresh snow would help or hurt his chances, but either way, he wanted nothing more than to find his buck.

At 5 a.m., he was at his stand, impatiently awaiting daylight. He began searching where he'd hit the buck, and then searched a willow thicket adjacent to the area. Next, he looked in a logged area that was full of brushy treetops, but still found no deer sign. Jantzi was now about 300 yards from where he'd shot the buck the night before.

Remembering that wounded deer often seek water, Jantzi decided to check a small spring, where he found deer tracks in the new snow.

After following the tracks for a while, he found blood in one of the tracks. When he brushed the snow away, he discovered a large puddle of blood among some fluffed-up leaves.

Judging by the size of the puddle, Jantzi was confident he'd soon find the buck. Finally, things were looking up.

Jantzi returned to the spring, and searched the other side. There he found more scuffed leaves, but no blood. Now Jantzi was confused.

After staring at the leaves for a while, he stood up to resume his search, and 10 yards away he saw his dead buck — the biggest buck he had ever seen.

The 10-pointer field dressed at 225 pounds, and netted 129 2/8 inches.

Father Fondly Recalls Son's Only Big Buck

One golden fall morning will always stick out in Henry Brosch's mind as a bittersweet memory.

It was the morning his son, Dolan, shot his first, and only, whitetail with a bow and arrow. But it was so much more than that.

Brosch and his son hunted together frequently, but on that particular morning, for some reason, Brosch decided to sleep in.

Brosch had spotted a small 8-pointer on two occasions right behind the house, but that morning, fate brought Dolan an even bigger buck.

HUNTER: **Dolan Brosch**
DATE: **October, 1999**
LOCATION: **Pennsylvania**
METHOD: **Bow**
RACK: **8-point buck**

When Dolan couldn't roust his father out of bed to go hunting, he went by himself. His father said he'd join him in a while, but he was still in bed when Dolan returned home only 15 minutes later.

Dolan woke up his father, telling him he'd shot a nice buck with his bow.

The elder Brosch couldn't believe his son could shoot a buck in 15 minutes, especially with a bow, but he got up and went to investigate, and within minutes he was helping drag his son's first bow-killed buck back to the house.

After that, Brosch made sure he got up every morning to go hunting, but he didn't get a deer that season.

What's worse, hunting time together for father and son was limited.

Dolan was diagnosed with testicular cancer and was treated with chemotherapy. The treatment killed the cancer, but it also burned his lungs, and unfortunately, the doctors didn't realize this complication until it was too late.

Dolan died shortly after doctors discovered the complication with his treatment.

And now, for Brosch, the memory of the time spent together bow-hunting with his son and especially the day Dolan shot his only bow-killed buck, is even more special.

Jim Phillips
Northeastern Wisconsin, 2001
120-class buck

Hunter Bags Best Buck, Then Bests Own Record

2002 was a year filled with big bucks for Roger Huff of Evansville, Ind.

On opening morning of Indiana's modern gun season, Huff made it to the woods late. Instead of making for his intended stand, he changed plans and opted to hunt along a field edge. The rut was in full swing, and from this new site, he would have the wind in his face.

As light filtered through the trees, Huff saw what appeared to be a buck bedded about 30 yards away. He scoped the deer, and saw that it carried a good-sized rack. Huff couldn't believe the deer hadn't spooked. Something wasn't right. Finally, rifle in hand, Huff approached the buck. When he drew nearer, he saw the buck was dead, and he soon found out why. An area of ground 25 feet by 25 feet had been obliterated. Another buck had killed this deer, puncturing its carotid artery. It couldn't have been dead for more than a half-hour.

As Huff left the field to get a road-kill tag for the dead buck, he saw a big buck chasing a doe across a field, but it was too far to shoot.

And that's the way the rest of the rifle season went. Huff saw plenty of bucks, but the big ones were always too far.

Huff took a break from Indiana's season to hunt Kentucky's rifle season opener.

Huff's Kentucky hunt was short and sweet. He saw a 10-pointer with a 19-inch spread chasing three does out of a thicket and across a pasture, and dropped it with his .270. It was the same deer his brother-in-law had captured on video. It was also Huff's biggest buck. But it wouldn't keep that title for long.

ROGER HUFF found this buck on opening day of gun season. The buck was killed by another buck.

Huff returned to Indiana and hunted hard for the rest of the gun season. Huff prefers late-season hunting because of the reduced hunting pressure, but the season expired before he could tag a buck.

Huff was excited for the muzzleloader season, which was another chance for him to enjoy the woods without other hunters around.

The rut was now essentially over, and Huff switched to hunting feeding areas in the evening.

On Dec. 12, he arrived at a field edge a bit late. The wind was in his favor, so he sat on the ground.

Soon, several does and satellite bucks entered the winter wheat field. The young bucks tried to breed the unreceptive does, and Huff enjoyed their antics.

About a half-hour before shooting light faded, a nice 10-pointer entered the field. Huff was about to shoot the buck when he noticed another deer entering the field. A 13-pointer joined the 10-pointer. The sight of the big bucks silhouetted against the pink and orange sunset was the most impressive sight Huff has ever seen in nature.

HUNTER: **Roger Huff**
DATE: **Opening Week 2002**
LOCATION: **Kentucky**
METHOD: **.270 Rifle**
RACK: **10-point buck**

Adrenaline surged as he dropped to the prone position for the 125-yard shot.

At the shot, the 13-pointer fell, and then got up and ran with the 10-pointer toward the woods. As Huff reloaded, he saw the deer stop, and then the 13-pointer fell again.

Huff hurried to the buck. However, when he was 20 feet away, the buck leaped up and ran. Huff fired again, but the buck made it into the woods and disappeared.

Huff went home to enlist a friend's help, and when they returned after nightfall, they recovered Huff's 13-pointer, which replaced the 10-pointer he had shot in Kentucky just days earlier as his best buck.

HUNTER: **Roger Huff**
DATE: **Dec. 12, 2002**
LOCATION: **Indiana**
METHOD: **Muzzleloader**
RACK: **13-point buck**

New York Hunter Tags 21-Point Nontypical

John Ballam of Prattsburgh, N.Y., never shot an arrow on his most memorable bow-hunt.

About an hour before sunset, he spotted a small buck coming toward him. When the deer was about 45 yards away, it bedded down. As Ballam watched the buck, another buck approached the bedded deer. As the second buck neared, the bucks stared at each other.

HUNTER: **John Ballam**
DATE: **2002**
LOCATION: **New York**
METHOD: **Gun**
RACK: **21-point buck**

Deer were everywhere, it seemed, when a doe tore through the woods before stopping 30 yards from Ballam's stand. The doe periodically watched its back trail, and because the rut was in full swing, Ballam hoped a large buck was pursuing the doe.

Ballam was right. The bruiser stopped about 40 yards out and stared at the doe. Then, yet another buck appeared. The latest arrival was an 8-pointer, but Ballam had his heart set on the heavy-beamed nontypical, which was trailing the doe.

Suddenly, the doe bolted into the woods, and the two largest bucks gave chase. The doe ran back out into the open, but Ballam couldn't see the big nontypical until he noticed a small tree violently swinging back and forth. The big buck was raking its antlers on the tree and pawing the ground like an enraged bull.

The two small bucks watched the nontypical for a while, and then ran. The doe followed, and the big nontypical chased after the doe.

The deer were gone, and Ballam's heart was racing.

Ballam hunted hard for the remainder of bow-season without seeing the big nontypical.

The weather for the first two days of shotgun season was the worst weather Ballam had encountered during deer season in years. He had limited hunting opportunities, and by the end of the second day, he still hadn't seen a deer.

On the third day, the weather improved, and Ballam saw a doe soon after first light. Trailing the doe was a big buck.

It took four shots, but Ballam dropped the buck. He excitedly hurried to it, and that's when he discovered his deer was the big nontypical he'd seen during bow-season.

Ballam's nontypical sported 21 points.

Out-of-State Hunt Yields Bow-Hunter's Best Buck

Tom Groller of Palmerton, Pa., took his annual bow-hunting trip to Ohio during the first week of November 2002. While the hunt is always enjoyable, this time, it was truly memorable.

Hunting was slow for most of the week, and Groller only saw a few deer. The bucks he saw were all small, and he passed on them, hoping a bigger deer would come his way as rutting activity increased.

On Nov. 9, the second-to-last day of his hunt, Groller arrived at his stand extra early to prepare his site.

His stand was situated in a funnel that usually has good deer sign each year. Groller doctored his mock scrape, which was positioned 50 yards from his stand, and laid some scent trails with a drag rag leading into his shooting lanes.

HUNTER: **Tom Groller**
DATE: **Nov. 9, 2002**
LOCATION: **Ohio**
METHOD: **Bow**
RACK: **9-point buck**

About 7:15 a.m., Groller grunted, and almost immediately, he heard a deer coming in his direction.

A buck walked into the scrape, thrashing the low-hanging branch. It then stood on its hind legs and did the same to the upper branches. The first thing Groller noticed was the buck's wide spread.

After the buck worked the scrape for a few minutes, it picked up one of Groller's scent trails and walked to Groller's stand as if it were on a fishing line.

The buck presented a broadside shot at 12 yards, and Groller's body and mind went into autopilot as he instinctively drew his bow, aimed and released his arrow.

The buck ran 40 yards and fell within sight of Groller's tree stand.

Groller's wide-racked buck had nine points and one broken brow tine. The rack stretched $21^1/_2$ inches across the beams.

The trophy 9-pointer, Groller's best buck to date, is destined for his wall to forever remind him of his magical Ohio morning in 2002.

Jim Crumley
Illinois, November 2002
150-class 9-pointer

Alberta Hunt Yields Buck of a Lifetime

Gary Jamieson of Honesdale, Pa., learned two lessons on his 1998 Alberta deer hunt: First, the size of Alberta bucks lives up to the hype, and second, persistence really does pay off.

Jamieson is normally a meat hunter, but on his Canadian adventure, he decided to hold out for a buck that would score at least 180 inches.

HUNTER: **Gary Jamieson**
DATE: **Nov. 20,1998**
LOCATION: **Alberta**
METHOD: **7 mm Rifle**
RACK: **21-point buck, 220-class**

Nov. 20 was the 14th and final day of Jamieson's hunt. His three companions had each filled their tags, and while they had shot good-sized bucks, they weren't the caliber of deer Jamieson was after. He'd traveled a long way for his hunt, and he wasn't about to settle for anything below his elevated standards.

As time raced by on the final day of the hunt, Jamieson's hopes of tagging an Alberta monarch had faded, and he started to realize that "the only thing heavier than a full game bag is an empty one."

Jamieson's guides told him there was just enough time for one last push through the bush, so they worked their way through dense cover while Jamieson watched a sprawling field where he'd seen some does cross earlier that day.

About 45 minutes into the drive, Jamieson saw movement at the far end of the field. A huge lone whitetail stepped into the open.

Jamieson used his rangefinder to determine the giant was 440 yards away. It was a long shot, but it was now or never.

Jamieson shouldered his 7 mm Rem. Mag loaded with handloaded bullets.

He put the cross hairs a few inches over the big buck's shoulder and gently tightened his finger around the trigger.

Jamieson couldn't tell whether he'd hit the buck, so he fired another round as the buck turned back into the bush.

When Jamieson reached the far end of the field, he found a good blood trail, and after following it 75 yards, he found his incredible buck. The first shot pierced the buck's lungs and the second shot hit a bit further back.

Jamieson's monstrous 21-pointer had a 28-inch spread and grossed 227 inches. The Canadian monster field dressed at 325 pounds.

Swap Hunt Results In Huge Iowa Nontypical

Sometimes the old "I'll scratch your back, and you scratch mine" adage works out pretty well.

At least Pete Geiger, of Withee, Wis., thinks so.

Geiger shot a 500-pound black bear in northern Wisconsin, and told his friend, Chad, who lives in Iowa.

Chad, a teacher by trade, had become friends with a farmer whose son was in his class. Chad told the farmer and his son about Geiger's bear, and they were so excited, you'd think they'd shot it.

HUNTER: **Pete Geiger**
DATE: **2002**
LOCATION: **Iowa**
METHOD: **Bow**
RACK: **18-point buck, 190-class**

One thing led to another, and soon Geiger was invited to Iowa to hunt whitetails on the farm.

On the first evening of his hunt, Geiger saw no deer.

On the second morning, he hunted from the same stand. It was extremely windy, and Geiger had a hard time hearing the doe that appeared at about 6:15 a.m.

An hour later, a huge nontypical sneaked in. Geiger first saw it when it was 40 yards away, and instantly noticed the buck's double drop tines.

The buck walked toward Geiger, making things seem too easy. When the buck was behind a tree, Geiger drew his bow and made an easy 15-yard shot.

The buck ran about 80 yards before collapsing.

In hindsight, Geiger was thankful the wind had masked the buck's presence. Geiger's knees were shaking so badly, he's sure he'd have missed the buck if he'd had more time to think about shooting it.

When Geiger showed the farmer his giant nontypical, Geiger was shocked to learned that he hadn't shot "the big buck." The farmer had seen an even larger buck in the area. It was then that Geiger realized just how incredible this slice of hunting heaven was.

Two points were broken off the buck's rack, but the remaining 18 points tallied 198⅞ nontypical inches.

The farmer's son is currently building preference points for a Wisconsin bear hunt, and Chad and the farmer are hoping to get in on the action too.

Delaware Hunter Slugs 12-Point Dream Buck

Standing hunters are supposed to get the shots during deer drives, but try telling that to a wily old buck. The unpredictable nature of mature white-tailed bucks means drivers must be equally ready at all times.

Francis Balback was ready as he walked during a drive on opening day of Delaware's 2002 shotgun deer season.

Balback, his son, Stephen, and a friend were hunting at Bombay Hook National Wildlife Refuge. The morning hunt was uneventful, so they decided to make drives through several fingers of woods in the afternoon.

On the first drive, Stephen walked while the other two posted. However, no one saw a deer.

HUNTER: **Francis Balback**
DATE: **Opening Day 2002**
LOCATION: **Delaware**
METHOD: **Shotgun**
RACK: **12-point buck, 170-class**

On the second drive, Francis volunteered to do the walking.

As he entered the small woods, he jumped a deer, but couldn't see it because the cover was too thick.

Francis continued through the woods, walking along a well-used deer trail. He came to the edge of the woods and pushed through thick cover as the woods gave way to a marsh.

Standing next to a stream about 40 yards away was a large doe.

Balback snapped his scoped 12-gauge to his shoulder and was about to shoot when he noticed movement behind the doe.

Very slowly, a big buck stood up.

Francis moved the cross hairs off the doe and onto the buck's shoulder and shot. The bruiser buck collapsed.

The 12-pointer had a 17-inch spread and grossed $175\frac{5}{8}$ inches. The buck dressed out at 192 pounds.

The buck is the largest buck Francis has shot, and he was understandably happy after shooting his dream buck.

If there is a downside to his story, however, it is the fact that he was about a mile and a half from his vehicle when he shot his trophy buck.

Bow-Hunter Arrows Kansas Nontypical

My bow-hunting partner, Ron, and I traveled to Kansas in 2002 for our fourth annual Kansas bow-hunt.

Our friend, Les, informed us that some local hunters had spotted a 200-class nontypical buck in the area we hunt.

After a long day of scouting on Monday, Ron and I missed the evening bow-hunt to place two new stands. As things turned out, that was the most beneficial night of missed bow-hunting we've ever had.

Dawn broke crisp and clear on Nov. 6. Four hours had passed quickly on stand, even though it had been an uneventful morning. Then, a loud grunt penetrated the morning silence. I stood up and got ready. Another grunt came from the cedars in front of me, and this time I saw a body moving quickly. Soon the buck appeared, and I was astounded by its antler size and mass.

HUNTER: **Lance Black**
DATE: **Nov. 6, 2002**
LOCATION: **Kansas**
METHOD: **Bow**
RACK: **19-point buck, 210-class**

The buck angled away from me at a steady gait. I wondered what I should do to turn this buck. I had an estrous bleat call, a grunt call and a rattling bag to work with. I grabbed my bleat call first. The buck stopped and looked back, but it soon began moving away again. The buck was now 80 to 90 yards away. I grunted, but the deer kept moving. I grunted louder and it stopped and looked back. I grunted loudly again, and the buck turned and came straight at me. My heart jumped and pounded as I fought to control my breathing.

The buck continued straight at me and closed the distance quickly. At about 35 yards, I drew my bow, thinking the buck wasn't going to stop. As I came to full draw, it stopped straight on and right behind a tree. I held the bow at full draw for what seemed like an eternity, mentally pleading the buck to move. Finally, I couldn't hold the bow any longer, and as slowly as possible, I let off.

The buck stood behind the tree for a couple of minutes. I wanted it to move to the west, which would keep it from smelling me. Instead, it walked straight south, positioning itself directly downwind of me.

After a couple of steps it locked up like a bird dog on point, and I knew it smelled me. It was now or never, and luckily the buck stopped where there was a small hole in the brush to place a shot. I released the arrow, hitting the buck in the middle of its body, but slightly behind where I aimed.

After the buck was out of sight, I thanked the Lord and my dad, God rest his soul.

My mind raced and I mentally played the shot over and over. It looked like it was hit hard. Did I hit it where I thought I did?

I got down and quietly moved to where the buck was standing when I shot. I immediately found my arrow, which had passed through the buck and was covered with good blood. My heart pounded with excitement, and after studying the arrow, I knew I had made a solid hit. I marked the spot and quietly left.

Ron had arrived at the truck a couple of minutes before me. He had killed a 7-pointer with an 18-inch spread. We celebrated with some high fives as we relished the thought of getting a Kansas double on two mature whitetails.

We decided to give my buck two hours before going after it. Based on the liver shot I thought I had made, we felt two hours was sufficient.

The day was warming fast and there was a steady 10 to 15 mph wind when we went to look for my buck. This made for tough tracking because the blood had dried, and the buck was bleeding mostly inside. Although the blood trail was sparse, there was enough to keep us going.

Ron found where the buck had gone through some small brush and had wiped blood off both sides of its body. We were moving into a cedar draw, and I scanned the trees for any sign of the buck. I was starting to get a little nervous because of the lack of blood. However, before I took another step, I spotted the buck's antlers sticking up from a depression in the cedars.

"There he is," I whispered.

All he could say is "Oh my God!"

After carefully moving in and confirming the buck was dead, we gasped and were in awe at what was before us. The buck was truly a once-in-a-lifetime deer, with 19 scorable points, unbelievable mass and tines that were truly indescribable.

After field dressing the awesome buck and dragging it back to the truck, we loaded it up and headed into town to show Les. Les came around the truck and said, "You got him," referring to the 200-class buck the local hunters had spotted.

The buck officially scored 213 2/8 nontypical. It is truly an awesome deer, and I will be forever grateful to have had a great confidant and hunting partner along with me to share the experience.

— Lance Black

PETE ROHE shot this 11-pointer while visiting relatives. The 150-class buck had the mass and tines Rohe had dreamed of when picturing a perfect deer.

5

A Family Affair

Dream Buck Makes Holiday Extra Special

Pete Rohe of Neenah, Wis., traveled with his family to visit his in-laws in southwestern Wisconsin for Thanksgiving in 2002. An avid deer hunter, Rohe hoped to do a little hunting on his brother-in-law's land during his holiday visit.

Rohe's brother-in-law practices quality deer management on his property, and shot a nice 13-pointer two days before Rohe arrived. He told Rohe he could shoot any doe or a buck at least 2½ years old.

Rohe and his brother-in-law scouted the land and hung a stand in a big white oak.

The next morning, Rohe returned. He saw a doe and a buck fawn.

That evening, the wind picked up, and when he awoke the next morning, it was howling. Rohe thought about sleeping in and taking the day off from hunting, but decided he'd much rather be outside than sitting around inside thinking about hunting, even if it was miserable weather. So, he braved the 25 mph wind and 15-degree temperature and headed for his stand.

Rohe was on stand an hour before first light, and by 8 a.m., he was shivering. He decided to tough it out until 8:30 before taking a walk through the area to warm up.

At 8:05 he used a bleat can, and minutes later, two does appeared. Rohe hoped a buck would follow them.

Rohe had watched the does for a few minutes, when one of the does suddenly looked over its shoulder. Rohe instantly spotted a buck. Although he just caught a glimpse of its antlers, he knew it was big.

The does were walking away from the buck, and Rohe knew the buck would follow. He looked for a shooting lane in the direction the buck was traveling, and waited.

Finally the buck ran after the does, and Rohe readied himself for a shot. The buck passed through Rohe's shooting lane too fast for a shot, but stopped moments later. Part of the buck's vitals were obscured, but Rohe had a good shot at the buck's front shoulder. He fired and the buck ambled 30 yards before going down.

The 150-class 11-pointer was the buck Rohe had always dreamed of.

WITH HELP from his brother and mother, Jason Maddy recovered this 8-pointer with a 24-inch spread the morning after he shot it.

Iowa Hunter Tracks Down Wide 8-Pointer

The lack of snow in Winter 2002 made recovering a buck extra hard for an Iowa hunter.

Jason Maddy was hunting during Iowa's late muzzleloader season Jan. 2, 2002. As he sat, he heard crashing nearby that sounded like "a freight train in the timber." Soon a doe emerged with an 8-pointer in tow. Maddy figured the buck had been trying to roust the doe from its bed.

The buck chased the doe across a creek, and Maddy planned to shoot the buck in the openness of the creek, but the buck vaulted across it in a single leap.

In his excitement, Maddy breathed on his scope, fogging it.

Maddy finally got his chance when the buck was 60 yards away. Maddy fired and the buck fell.

Darkness fell 10 minutes later, so Maddy climbed down from his stand and walked to his buck. However, when Maddy reached the spot where the buck fell, he discovered the deer had disappeared.

Maddy returned home and decided to track the buck on the snowless ground in the morning.

At 8 a.m., Maddy returned, along with his brother, Keane, and their mother.

There was no blood, and things weren't looking promising. Finally, as the morning sun began to melt the frost, small splotches of blood became visible.

The tracking grew painstaking. The group had only covered 200 yards in three hours. Keane circled ahead and found a big puddle of blood 50 yards ahead. Then, 10 yards away, the buck stood up. The hunt was over with one well-placed shot.

Maddy's original shot hit the buck high on the shoulder, breaking both front shoulders, yet the buck still went 200 yards.

The 8-pointer had a 24-inch inside spread and dressed at more than 250 pounds.

Challenge Leads to Father-Son Moment

Clay Atkinson of Barrie, Ontario, has hunted whitetails with gun and crossbow for more than 20 years. In 2001, his uncle told him that the ultimate challenge was to shoot a mature buck with a bow, so in 2002, Atkinson accepted his uncle's challenge and bought a compound bow.

Atkinson practiced every day during the summer, and soon was placing his arrows in the bull's-eye out to 40 yards.

Although Atkinson was confident in his shooting skill, a month and a half into the bow season, he still hadn't been able to use it.

Finally, on Nov. 19, Atkinson got his chance.

HUNTER: **Clay Atkinson**
DATE: **Nov. 19, 2002**
LOCATION: **Ontario**
METHOD: **Bow**
RACK: **8-point buck**

He and his father were bow-hunting 90 yards apart that morning. Just after sunrise, Atkinson heard a twig snap, and his heart beat heavily. Five minutes later he spotted movement.

Two deer were moving toward his stand, and as they drew nearer, Atkinson identified them as a doe and a small 6-point buck. When their heads went behind a small pine 25 yards away, Atkinson drew his bow.

When the deer stepped clear of the tree, Atkinson looked the buck over. He wanted his first buck with a bow to be a big one, but it took every ounce of his willpower not to shoot. With mixed emotions, he let the buck pass. The deer walked past the elder Atkinson's stand, and with the same indecision, he too, finally decided to let the buck go.

The longer Atkinson sat, the more he second-guessed his decision. However, an hour and a half later, another deer appeared.

It was a nice 8-pointer, and it was on the same trail as the first deer. Atkinson drew again as the buck passed behind the pine, and after it cleared, he shot. The buck bounded off and fell within sight.

His father, who Atkinson had momentarily forgotten, yelled, "You got him!" Then father and son assembled around Atkinson's memorable 8-pointer.

Father and Son Shoot New York Trophies

The 2001 and 2002 deer seasons resulted in a pair of big bucks for a New York father-son duo.

Mike Kubacki and his son, Mike Jr., of Central Square, N.Y., were excited for the 2001 bow-season. It would be Mike Jr.'s first hunting season.

However, the Kubackis saw little deer activity early in the season, and their enthusiasm waned. Mike Jr. began skipping hunts or sleeping in, leaving his father to go it alone.

The elder Kubacki was regularly seeing does and a pair of spike bucks, but nothing he wanted to shoot.

HUNTER: **Mike Kubacki**
DATE: **Nov. 4, 2001**
LOCATION: **New York**
METHOD: **Bow**
RACK: **8-point buck**

On Nov. 3, he got off of work in time to hunt out of his son's stand behind the house. The wind was ideal, and it was time for bucks to be on the move.

That evening a small 8-pointer appeared, but somehow it sensed the hunter perched in a tree and disappeared.

Disappointed, Kubacki placed buck urine near the stand the next morning to try to convince the next buck to linger a little longer and hopefully present a shot.

After three hours on stand that morning Kubacki had seen five does, and was disappointed when he didn't see a buck. He was about to climb down when he heard hoofsteps. An enraged 8-pointer emerged. The hair stood on the buck's neck as it snorted, wheezed and pawed the ground. Kubacki had never seen a show like this.

Suddenly, Kubacki realized the buck was on a trail that would pass only 5 yards from his stand. When the angry buck reached that point, Kubacki shot, hitting the buck.

Kubacki had to cling to the tree after arrowing the 8-pointer. When he finally calmed down enough to leave his tree stand, he followed a short blood trail to his $3^{1}/_{2}$-year-old 8-pointer, which dressed at 201 pounds.

Kubacki's son was amazed by the buck, and both hunters had

renewed enthusiasm for the 2002 season.

It was Mike Jr.'s turn to bag the big one in 2002.

Mike Jr. got a shot at a 4-pointer with his bow. Although he missed it, the encounter kick-started his enthusiasm for deer hunting, and he talked non-stop about the buck that was almost his.

Opening day of the shotgun season was cold, snowy and windy. The Kubackis sat on stand for four hours, but that's all they could stand. They decided to put on a small drive for other family members before heading home.

To do the drive, the Kubackis had to skirt a small beaver pond, cross the beaver dam, then hike through a small block of woods.

HUNTER: **Mike Kubacki Jr.**
DATE: **Opening Day 2002**
LOCATION: **New York**
METHOD: **Shotgun**
RACK: **8-point buck**

The beaver dam was flooded, so they had to cross through thick cover behind it. When they reached the creek, they were looking for a good crossing site when Mike Jr. saw a deer standing statue-like only 20 yards away. Due to snow and ice on the tree branches, at first they didn't know what it was. Then Mike Jr. whispered, "It's a buck, Dad!"

Instantly he shouldered his 12 gauge and fired. The buck bounded off.

Mike Jr. tried to run after the deer, but his father stopped him with a hand on his shoulder.

"Calm down, calm down, I've never caught one yet," he said to his excited son.

But the elder Kubacki understood his son's feelings. When the deer took off, they both got a good look at the buck's tall, wide rack.

Mike Jr. began blood-trailing the buck, turning to his father every couple steps to tell him what had happened as if he wasn't there to see it.

After 70 yards of trailing, Mike Jr. was first to spot the fallen buck.

The back slaps from Mike Jr.'s father, uncles and cousins brought the group together in a memory they'd never forget. The 8-pointer had a 20-inch inside spread and field dressed at 153 pounds. Mike Jr.'s 2002 buck and his father's 2001 buck now hang side by side in their living room.

Indiana Clan Enjoys Amazing 2002 Season

The 2002 season was one to remember for four Indiana hunting partners. All four hunters tagged huge bucks.

Jon Ringer was the first to taste success. On Nov. 2, he awoke extra early to bow-hunt. He'd been saving his best stand for the rut, and finally, cold weather had arrived. It was time to hunt his ace-in-the-hole stand.

He met his brother, Timm, at their favorite spot at 6:30 a.m., then they headed to their stands, which were situated 150 yards apart.

HUNTER: **Jon Ringer**
DATE: **Nov. 2, 2002**
LOCATION: **Indiana**
METHOD: **Bow**
RACK: **9-point buck**

Ringer crawled into his stand at about 6:45 a.m. He had more than a half-hour to wait until legal shooting time.

Just as it was getting light, he heard a deer trotting toward him. Following the sound as best he could, soon he could make out a big shadow about 40 yards away, moving through the woods. Ringer strained to see antlers, and when the buck passed in front of a large beech, he saw high tines.

Ringer grabbed his bow, knocked an arrow and got ready. His heart pounded and his mind raced as he saw the rack more clearly. This buck was definitely a shooter!

As the deer drew closer, Ringer hoped there was enough light to aim his bow.

Ringer was already at full draw when the buck stepped into an opening 25 yards away. The buck stopped in the shooting lane, and Ringer was grateful he could see his sights, and sent his arrow on its way.

The arrow struck the buck with a solid "whack," then the buck kicked out its feet and crashed into the woods. Ringer heard the deer fall.

Ringer wanted to go see his deer, but decided to wait so he wouldn't ruin his brother's hunt. As luck would have it, another nice 8-pointer passed under his stand.

When Ringer met his brother at 8:45 a.m., his brother asked why he hadn't shot the 8-pointer.

"Because I shot a bigger one!" he replied.

The Ringer party's good fortune continued later in November, but it wasn't without mishaps.

Brandon Ringer had experienced nothing but hard luck earlier in the season. During bow-season, his bow developed a squeak when he drew, which scared deer. Next, the sight on his muzzleloader kept going out of line, and try as he might, he couldn't correct the problem. So, for the shotgun season, he toted the .410 that his father, Jon, had given him for his 14th birthday. It wasn't his weapon of choice, but it would have to suffice.

On Nov. 22, Ringer climbed into his father's tree stand at about 2 p.m. for an afternoon hunt. Things weren't going well. After a few hours he'd only seen one doe. But that wasn't the worst of it. At about 4:00, a neighbor drove his golf cart near Ringer's stand, checking out the property, and essentially scaring any deer in the area.

Seeing that things just kept getting worse the more he hunted, Ringer decided to end his hunt early. As he was walking out of the woods, he came to the trail he walks down when he goes to his own tree stand, and something told him he should go sit in his own stand for a while.

As he walked to his tree, he spooked four does.

He climbed into the stand, got settled in, and waited. After about a half-hour, he spotted a deer about 100 yards behind him. He couldn't tell what it was, but it was getting closer. When it raised its head, he saw points, and lots of them! When he counted five points on one side, he knew it was a really nice buck.

When the buck was about 70 yards away, it turned broadside and lifted its head.

Ringer raised the shotgun, but the bead behind the buck's shoulder, and fired. The buck ran 15 yards before falling.

Ringer's streak of bad luck had finally ended. The 10-pointer field dressed at 152 pounds, and is the biggest buck Ringer has ever shot.

HUNTER: **Brandon Ringer**
DATE: **Nov. 22, 2002**
LOCATION: **Indiana**
METHOD: **Shotgun**
RACK: **10-point buck**

On the second weekend of Indiana's 2002 shotgun season, it was David Thacker's turn to tag a buck. Thacker was hunting with his friend Rod Ringer.

The men were hunting about 150 yards apart and each carried radio a headset to keep in touch.

At about 7:30 a.m., Thacker spotted a doe about 100 yards away. He and Ringer conversed, asking each other if they'd seen the deer, and if there were any bucks following. They both saw it, but neither hunter could see any bucks trailing the doe.

An hour later, Thacker spotted two does running about 80 yards away. This time a nice buck was chasing them

Thacker radioed Ringer to report the news, but almost immediately, the does ran closer to Thacker's stand. He didn't have time to talk now. He had to shoot because the buck was 50 yards away and closing fast.

HUNTER: **David Thacker**
DATE: **2002**
LOCATION: **Indiana**
METHOD: **Shotgun**
RACK: **8-point buck**

"Did you say you saw a shooter?" Ringer asked.

At that moment, the buck raised its head, put its nose in the air and lip curled. Thacker centered the cross-hairs on the buck's shoulder, and his only response to Ringer's question was a single shot.

The buck stumbled and fell in a patch of thick cover.

"I guess you did see a shooter!" Ringer joked.

Thacker kept his eyes on the place he thought the buck fell, 15 yards from where it had stood when he shot.

Thacker climbed down from his stand and was on the way to look for his buck when he noticed something very unusual. There was blood on the deer trail just 5 yards from his stand. Could he have been so focused on the spot the buck fell that he'd missed it when it ran right past him? Thacker grew worried. The spot of blood was now a full-fledged trail. Still, he continued to where he saw the deer fall, and there he found the buck. It was the same deer that passed by too far during bow-season.

Because he'd hunted the same stand the night before and hadn't seen the blood, Thacker concluded a wounded deer must have ran past his stand during the night.

HUNTER: **Rod Ringer**
DATE: **2002**
LOCATION: **Indiana**
METHOD: **Muzzleloader**
RACK: **10-point buck**

Despite his companions' success, Rod Ringer's tag remained unfilled as deer season wore down. But a chance sighting helped him bag his buck.

Jon and Tami Ringer saw a nice buck one morning out their living room window. They briefly captured it on video before it disappeared.

The next morning Jon and Rod sat back to back, hoping to see the buck again. They heard one gun shot, but didn't think much of it. After an hour, they decided to go home for breakfast.

As they drove home, the same buck limped across the driveway in front of them. They turned around and the chase began.

The men found a faint blood trail in the scattered snow and tracked the buck to a river near where they'd spotted it the day before.

After losing the trail, Rod climbed into a high tree stand, hoping to spot the deer, but the buck was long gone. After some diligent searching, Jon picked up the trail again.

Jon and Rod drove back home to shed some layers before going back after the buck. They found where the buck had swam across the river and continued trailing it for about a mile before they finally spotted it bedded down in a tree line about 50 yards in front of them.

Rod fired his muzzleloader and the buck faltered before running over a hill and out of sight.

Rod excitedly ran after the deer, while Jon eased ahead. Seconds later rod exclaimed the buck was down.

When they examined Rod's big 10-pointer, they learned that the buck's right hoof was nearly severed, which had caused the blood trail.

Close inspection revealed that indeed, this buck was the same one the Ringers had videotaped from their living room the day before.

So with Rod's buck, the Ringer clan concluded its dream season. Although all four hunters had shot nice bucks before, they would have never dreamed they'd all shoot the big one in the same season.

Iowa Brothers Bag Pair of Trophy Bucks

Mention Iowa, and deer hunters immediately conjure up thoughts of hog-bodied whitetails with antlers to match. And that's exactly the kind of deer Kevin and Mike Muehlenkamp encountered on their 2002 hunts.

One week before bow-season, Kevin scouted a soybean field adjacent to a 10-year fallow field. To his surprise, he saw 20 does and seven bucks the first evening.

The next day he returned to find a spot to place his tree stand. The only suitable place was in a small elm in a fence line. He stuck out like a giant in the stand, but it was the only spot available.

HUNTER: **Kevin Muehlenkamp**
DATE: **2002**
LOCATION: **Iowa**
METHOD: **Bow**
RACK: **9-point buck**

The first night he hunted from the stand he saw several bucks, including a nice 9-pointer. However, the 9-pointer was too far, and Muehlenkamp forgot to bring his grunt call. He tried grunting with his mouth, and the deer approached. When it was 20 yards away, Muehlenkamp drew. Unfortunately, another buck moved in front of the big buck, and Muehlenkamp had no shot.

Muehlenkamp returned a few days later, and once again several does appeared, followed by several bucks. Suddenly the big 9-pointer returned, but this time it was behind Muehlenkamp. The buck walked toward Muehlenkamp, but Muehlenkamp couldn't move to get in position because there were so many deer around him and he couldn't risk spooking them.

When Muehlenkamp finally had a chance to shoot, the buck was right under his tree and only 3 yards away! Muehlenkamp shot, and the buck ran off.

Muehlenkamp found no blood trail, but he did see the arrow in the buck when it ran. He decided to search for the buck in the morning.

The next day Muehlenkamp returned with a large search party. They recovered the dead buck just inside a nearby woods.

Although it seemed like a strange spot for a stand, no one questioned it after seeing the monster buck!

After hearing Kevin's success story early in the bow-season, Kevin's brother, Mike, decided to hunt from Kevin's tree stand in the elm tree during Iowa's late muzzleloader season.

Mike also scouted just before the season opened. However, he noticed four old farm wagons in the area, and because he could shoot farther with his muzzleloader than Kevin could with his bow, he decided to hide behind the wagons instead of climbing into his brother's "exposed" tree stand.

While scouting that night, Mike was amazed at what he saw. Deer were everywhere! Mike counted more than 70 deer, including 21 bucks, with at least seven bucks he considered shooters.

HUNTER: **Mike Muehlenkamp**
DATE: **2002**
LOCATION: **Iowa**
METHOD: **Muzzleloader**
RACK: **10-point buck**

Mike called Kevin that night, bubbling with excitement. Kevin thought he was exaggerating when Mike excitedly related his tale. Kevin assumed that maybe Mike had seen half that many deer, but Mike knew what he'd seen. Plus, the shotgun season had just ended, and it made sense that deer would congregate in the lightly hunted area after being pressured by hunters.

After a couple days of hunting from his makeshift stand in the old wagons, Mike hadn't fired a shot. He'd seen plenty of bucks, however, and was confident in the area, considering all the deer he'd been seeing.

Just as he was about to leave his stand the second evening, Mike took one more look around the field. It was a good thing he did! He spotted a wide-racked 10-pointer just entering the field to feed.

Mike was surprised to see this buck because neither he nor any of his hunting partners had seen the deer before.

It didn't take Mike long to decide this buck was a shooter, and he shouldered his muzzleloader.

A well-placed shot dropped the thick-beamed 10-pointer, which sported a $23^{3}/_{4}$-inch outside spread.

Hunt is Special for Father and Son

HUNTER: **Patrick Moore Jr.**
DATE: **Opening Day 2002**
LOCATION: **Pennsylvania**
METHOD: **.45-70 Gov. Rifle**
RACK: **11-point buck**

The 2002 hunting season was a dream come true for Patrick Moore Jr. of Hegins, Pa.

Hunting at the family cabin, the Three Pt. Hunting Lodge, Moore and his son shot black bears within two minutes of each other. What's more, they saw several bucks, including two bruisers.

Moore lives on a small farm in prime deer country, but the thought of hunting big bucks in an undisturbed area (Moore's hunting spot is 4 miles from a blacktop road, plus 2 miles from camp) convinced him to head back to the lodge for gun season.

Moore's son decided to hunt at home with friends, but Moore's father agreed to join him.

On opening morning, the duo awoke at 4 a.m., and after scarfing down a hearty breakfast, they headed for their stands.

Along the way, they reminisced about bygone hunts with family and friends. They reached the fork in the trail too soon, and Moore's father split off for his stand while Moore continued another quarter-mile to the laurel ridge he and his son hunted during bear season.

From his vantage point 30 feet up in an old oak, Moore could see two laurel-covered benches.

Moore hoisted his grandfather's Model 1895 .45-70 Gov. into the stand, loaded it and prepared for his cold sit.

At about 7 a.m., he heard distant shots, but he hadn't cut a single human track, and he was sure he had the area to himself.

Minutes later, he saw a deer moving through the laurels, and seconds later he saw it was a nice buck. Moore picked an opening where the deer would cross about 75 yards away.

When the deer entered the opening, more placed the cross hairs on the buck and fired. The buck dropped, then got back up. Moore fired again and the deer was down for good.

Moore radioed his father, and both men were equally impressed when they reached the 11-pointer with a 19½-inch spread. After field dressing it, they began the long, satisfying walk to camp.

Dick Scorzafava
Missouri
16-pointer
245 pounds field dressed

Dick Scorzafava

Hunter Discovers Generosity of Strangers

The 2002 deer season was probably the most emotional season ever for Patrick Ludwig of Selinsgrove, Pa.

From frustration, to bliss, Ludwig experienced it all. And he also learned the generosity of strangers and the joy of family.

HUNTER: **Patrick Ludwig**
DATE: **2002**
LOCATION: **Pennsylvania**
METHOD: **.32 Win. Special**
RACK: **11-point buck**

Going into the season, Ludwig had not shot a buck in 27 years of hunting. Ludwig had scouted his hunting area in the summer and had bow-hunted the same area earlier in the season. He was only hoping for any legal deer for him and his father to put meat on the table.

On opening day, Ludwig missed two does, so he and his father decided to switch stands the second day. On Day 2, father and son hunted until 1 p.m. before meeting at the car to warm up and update each other on the morning's hunt.

At about 2:30 they took to the woods again, but they decided it would take too long for the elder Ludwig to reach his son's stand because he is diabetic and has a prosthetic leg. So each hunter returned to his respective stand.

At 3:45, Ludwig was praying for another chance at a deer when his prayers were answered in a big way. An 11-point buck appeared 30 yards away. Ludwig shouldered his .32 Win. Special, concentrated on breathing and aiming, and fired. The buck didn't know where the shot came from and stood for a moment before trotting off.

Ludwig fired again and the buck disappeared.

Ludwig couldn't believe he missed. He ran to where the buck had first stood and found nothing. He ran to the second spot, and again found nothing. Disappointment gripped him.

Ludwig ran to the edge of the woods to see if his father was coming. Indeed he was, along with his friend, Brother Miller.

Ludwig raced to the two men,

falling on his knees to catch his breath. After relating his story, all three men returned to where the buck was to examine their situation.

Ludwig's father found a shattered branch where Ludwig had fired his first shot. The trio walked to where the buck had crossed a creek 75 yards away, and Brother Miller found blood. The elder Ludwig noted it was dark red, indicating a probably liver hit. Ludwig yelled for joy, knowing it was a lethal shot.

Thinking the buck might still be in the area, the party stayed quiet and still for 10 minutes, then tried to follow the buck's blood trail.

As Ludwig scanned the woods, he saw the buck's antlers sticking up on the other side of the creek, but before he could shoot, the buck bounded away. Ludwig fired at the fleeing buck, which then disappeared.

Going on pure adrenaline, Ludwig crossed the knee-deep, 20-foot-wide creek. As he did, he saw the buck jump up and run deeper into the woods.

Ludwig examined the buck's bed and found a lot of blood, as did Brother Miller back on the opposite side of the creek. Ludwig's overwhelming excitement caused him to vomit!

As light faded and legal shooting time passed, the hunters decided to leave the buck until morning.

The following morning, Ludwig returned with his father and son, Dakota. The excited Ludwig sped down the trail, leaving his father and son behind.

The observers cut ahead about the time Ludwig lost the trail. Ludwig's father found blood, but this time it was bright red. He stood near the blood while Ludwig and Dakota carefully picked up the trail, eventually making it up to the elder Ludwig's position.

The trail now went up a steep hill, and Ludwig's father had extreme difficulty cresting it.

When they reached the summit, "no trespassing" signs were everywhere.

Ludwig saw a car parked along a road and approached. A woman stepped out and informed him she owned the land. After hearing his story, she permitted Ludwig to track his buck.

Ludwig went back to his family and took up the trail, and minutes later heard to shots about 30 seconds apart. His hopes sank, assuming someone had killed his buck.

Minutes later, the woman approached. She said she'd shot at a doe, when she noticed movement. Ludwig's buck was on the ground, too weak to get up, so she finished it. She told Ludwig to come tag his buck.

Ludwig couldn't believe it. He thanked her and got her name and address to send her a Christmas card. When he saw the deer, he was so excited he couldn't remember how to field dress it. Luckily, his family was there to help him and to share his excitement.

N.J. Hunter Brings In Odd-Antlered Whitetail

Robert LeDrew had a deer season to remember in 2002. He, his brothers and their sons have hunted state-owned pine barrens in New Jersey for more than 30 years, but they've never seen a buck as heavy, or as unusual, as the one LeDrew shot on opening day.

On opening morning, it was about 18 degrees, with 4 inches of frozen snow on the ground. It was very clear and quiet, but the frozen snow made traveling very noisy.

Less than 30 minutes after taking his stand, LeDrew heard a deer trotting toward him. It was about 150 yards away, and LeDrew could see the buck only because of the contrast of its dark body against the snow.

HUNTER: **Robert LeDrew**
DATE: **Opening Day 2002**
LOCATION: **New Jersey**
METHOD: **Shotgun**
RACK: **5-point buck**

When the buck stopped, LeDrew glassed it and saw a nice rack against the snow. When it stopped again 20 yards away, LeDrew had it covered with his 870 Wingmaster. The buck crumpled.

LeDrew didn't want to ruin the hunt for his brother, who was only 150 yards away, so he waited before retrieving his buck.

As he sat, he grew confused. When he'd first seen the deer, he was sure he'd seen antlers on both sides, but as he looked at the deer from his stand, he wasn't sure what to think. Finally, after 2 hours, LeDrew went to examine his deer.

He couldn't believe what he saw. The left antler was normal and sported four points, but the right antler was bizarre.

A single thick tine grew sideways out of the pedicle, then went straight down along its face between the ear and the eye before before curling out and straight up. In fact, the antler cut a U-shaped gouge out of the ear.

When LeDrew brought his buck to a taxidermist, he discovered that the buck had cracked its skull plate, and when the pedicle healed, it was tilted to the right.

The buck dressed at 130 pounds and is the largest LeDrew's group has ever shot.

Uncle and Nephew Share Memory, Deer Mount

Jim Kuhnle's father died when he was a toddler, so his uncle, Geoff Gilbertson, introduced him to hunting and fishing.

During Wisconsin's 2002 gun-season, uncle and nephew shared a hunt that strengthened the bond between them.

Kuhnle gets together with several relatives to conduct deer drives during the last three days of season. On the seventh day of the nine-day season, Kuhnle and the other drivers met before first light to discuss their plans for the day. Gilbertson had an appointment with his doctor and would show up later.

HUNTER: **Jim Kuhnle and Geoff Gilbertson**
DATE: **Nov. 29, 2002**
LOCATION: **Wisconsin**
METHOD: **Guns**
RACK: **9-point buck**

On the first drive, the hunters pushed several deer, but no one could tell if there were any bucks in the herd. But it didn't matter. All the deer ran into the mile-long stretch of woods the drivers planned to walk through on their next push.

Kuhnle posted at a fence post about 100 yards from the woods for the next drive. From his vantage point, he could shoot 300 yards in two directions.

Kuhnle expected the drive to last about 45 minutes, but 15 minutes into it, he heard about a half dozen deer running about 140 yards away, but he never saw them.

About 10 minutes later, Kuhnle heard Gilbertson's pickup, and uncle joined nephew for the remainder of the drive.

The two chatted a bit about the first drive and the deer that had just run out unseen. Then they joked about what would happen if a big buck ran out of the woods while they were standing together. They agreed they'd both claim the deer, and were still laughing about it, when ironically, a big buck did appear.

Both hunters emptied their guns, and when the shooting was over, the buck was dead.

They congratulated each other and went to examine the 9-pointer, which sported a 20-inch inside spread.

Not once did they question who the deer belonged to. They split the cost of mounting the buck, and now the mount spends equal time in their homes.

Faith Unlocks the Door to Big Whitetails

It was a warm autumn day in northwest Missouri — the third day of the firearms deer-hunting season. We had all hunted the preceding two days to no avail. I had taken up deer hunting with our two sons several years earlier after my husband, Lloyd, was incapacitated following a farm accident.

Fall was always my favorite season. I liked getting out in the timber tramping through leaves a new-fallen snow and seeing the birds, squirrels, rabbits and white-tailed deer. In northwest Missouri in the 1960s and '70s deer were scarce, then they finally made a population surge in the '80s.

HUNTER: **Vandora Willson**
DATE: **Nov. 16, 1981**
LOCATION: **Missouri**
METHOD: **.30-30 Rifle**
RACK: **8-point buck**

I started out hunting with Lloyd's 12-gauge semi-automatic shotgun, but it was a pretty heavy gun. One season I got a shot at a big 8- or 10-point buck coming right at me, but missed him. My oldest son, Darrell, told me that was the hardest shot to make, and even though I was sick about missing, I didn't give up. Lloyd took me to St. Joseph one day and bought me a Marlin .30-30 lever-action rifle. We also bought a 4x32 All-Pro rifle scope and had it mounted and sighted in by a specialist. I target practiced. Now I was ready to hunt white-tailed deer with my sons.

Several years later with a few small deer — some antlered, two or three button bucks and a spike buck to my credit, I was geared up for something bigger. On this particular Monday morning, Nov. 16, 1981, I had a week's laundry to tackle. We were hosting a revival at our church in Barnard that week and I was scheduled to sing a solo for the Monday night special music. I had chosen "Prayer is the Key to Heaven, But Faith Unlocks the Door."

As I went from the basement out to the clothesline with each basket of clothes to hang on the line, I practiced my song. I looked out across the 16-acre knoll of our farm each trip and would think to myself, "I'm going to see a big buck go across that field this morning." I didn't.

After we had finished our lunch and had cleared the table, Lloyd said, "Let's go check the cattle." I said I was too tired and we should rest first. He said, "No, let's check the cattle first, then rest."

We took our guns, got in the pickup and headed for the far back pasture. Everything seemed OK and we headed back for the house and our rest. As we rounded a corner and could see the knoll, Lloyd yelled, "There goes a deer and it's a buck!"

It was running by leaps and bounds.

"Stop and let me get out," I shouted.

I jumped out, braced myself against the door and shot, but missed. This was about a 150- to 200-yard shot.

Lloyd shouted, "You shot right behind him. Lead him more!"

So I shot again and this time I hit him in the hind quarter just below the spine. He stumbled but he got up and went on a little farther, then laid down in some tall grass with only his head and neck visible.

We both knew by the hunter's rule of thumb you are to leave a wounded deer lay and it will get stiff or bleed to death. However, we were both at such a high point by now that we thought I had to finish him off. After three more attempts, each time the deer jumping up and running farther across the farm, I hit him in the neck and he died after he crossed the river.

We had to have help to get him back across the river and in the pickup. We headed for the check station and checked him in, then went home and strung him up. Now it was time to do the evening chores and get ready for church. Still no rest!

When I got up in front of the filled-to-capacity church to sing my song, I announced that my message in song was "Prayer is the Key to Heaven, But Faith Unlocks the Door." I said, "You have to have faith. I had faith all morning that I would see a deer, and I did see one going across our field at 1:30 this afternoon in that very spot where I had looked all morning. I got him — an 8-point buck, a 200-yard shot."

There was some whispering in the audience. Several people did not even know I hunted.

Now, 20 years later, I tell my grandchildren this story. I remember it as though it were yesterday. Lloyd died 10 years ago, but our three grandsons like to hunt with us now. The grandsons have each experienced the thrill of seeing and shooting a big deer on their first day of hunting, and there will be many more thrills and memories, I am sure. Even the granddaughters and daughters-in-law get an urge to go with us sometimes.

We all love the venison steak and when the family comes to Grandma Willson's house for a meal, it's usually a rounded-up platter of venison steak, cooked with my special recipe, of course, and served with potatoes, gravy, vegetables and dessert.

I am 82 years old, and I am not the gal I used to be. I tell my sons, ages 49 and 41, every year at the close of the season, "This will probably be the last time I hunt with you."

They always laugh, give me a pat on the back, and say, "Oh, come on, Tutta, you'll be right out here again next year. We couldn't hunt without you."

So who knows what November 2003 will be like. We'll see.

— Vandora Willson

Gary Clancy
Montana
Velvet-antlered buck

Gary Clancy

Father's Advice Leads to Big Buck

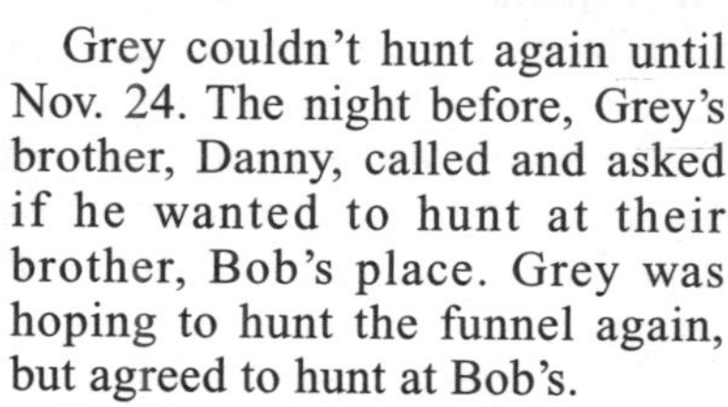

Donald Grey Jr., of Ticonderoga, N.Y., had hunted a big buck for several years, but somehow the buck always gave him the slip.

HUNTER: **Donald Grey Jr. (left)**
DATE: **Nov. 24, 2001**
LOCATION: **New York**
METHOD: **Gun**
RACK: **10-point buck**

In 2001, he saw the buck during the early bow season. The buck was too far away, but stayed in the area for 2 hours. Grey didn't see the buck for the rest of bow season.

Rifle season started unsuccessfully. Grey didn't see a deer on opening day. He decided to ask his father's advice.

Grey's father had a stroke and hasn't hunted for years, but his son has great respect for his woodsmanship. He told his son that the big buck he'd been seeing regularly crossed the road about a half-mile from his house. He recommended that his son hunt a funnel in the area and try to call the buck in with grunts and rattling.

On Nov. 15, Grey headed to the funnel, planning to sit all day if necessary. Grey hung out some scent wafers, and 15 minutes after sunrise, rattled and grunted. Suddenly a 5-pointer charged in, and Grey dropped it. His father's advice had been dead on, and Grey went to his father's house and gave him a big hug.

Grey couldn't hunt again until Nov. 24. The night before, Grey's brother, Danny, called and asked if he wanted to hunt at their brother, Bob's place. Grey was hoping to hunt the funnel again, but agreed to hunt at Bob's.

By 10:30 a.m., no one had seen anything at Bob's, so Danny and Donald left. Danny asked if Donald wanted to be dropped off at the funnel. Donald didn't know if he'd see anything, but he decided to give it a try.

It was a good thing he did.

He reached the cedar tree where he'd stood when he shot the 5-pointer, set up his scents and organized his calls. He rattled and mixed in a few grunts, and had barely put down the calls before the big 10-pointer he'd hunted for so long appeared. Grey concentrated on his shot and the buck dropped on the rifle's report.

Grey was so excited he ran a half-mile to Danny's house for help dragging his buck. After retrieving the buck, they drove to their father's house, where Grey embraced his father with tears in his eyes and thanked him for sharing his expert advice.

Boys Recover Big Buck On Their First Deer Hunt

Steve Wineman of New Palestine, Ind., fondly remembers the excitement he felt when his father prepared his hunting gear for opening day of deer season. Wineman enjoyed going along on the hunts and doing "man stuff," even though he never shot a deer in 10 years of trying.

Wineman quit deer hunting for a few years, but when his sons, Tyler and Kody were old enough to tag along, he wanted to show them the same excitement he felt as a child.

After years without toting a gun into the woods, Wineman readied his gear for opening day of the 2002 season.

HUNTER: **Steve Wineman**
DATE: **Opening Day 2002**
LOCATION: **Indiana**
METHOD: **Shotgun**
RACK: **13-point buck**

After donning plenty of warm clothes, the Wineman crew hit the woods. The boys were filled with questions, and Wineman patiently answered them to the best of his ability.

The boys did a good job of staying quiet and motionless on stand. At 7:30, three does walked through the woods undisturbed, but Wineman didn't have a doe tag. He hoped a buck would follow their trail.

Time passed slowly, and the crew grew cold. Wineman decided i' time to take a break and me hot cocoa and potato

en, a stick snapped hind them. The Winemans froze, and a nice buck materialized.

The buck hadn't detected Wineman and his sons, and Wineman reached for his shotgun. However, the buck saw the excited hunter move, and looked straight at Wineman.

Wineman snapped up the shotgun and took a hasty shot at the buck, missing it. The buck bounded down a ravine and out of sight. Then, it emerged going up the other side of the hill about 75 yards away. Wineman fired twice more, and although the buck kept running, Wineman was sure that he hit it.

Wineman waited 5 minutes, then the crew went looking for the buck. They found the 13-point, 225-pound buck about 125 yards away.

Hunt For Indiana Buck is a Family Effort

HUNTER: **Rick Laney**
DATE: **Opening Day 2001**
LOCATION: **Indiana**
METHOD: **Shotgun**
RACK: **9-point buck**

Sometimes incidents stick out in your memory. The sighting of a huge buck was one such incident for Kyle Laney of Bloomingdale, Ind.

Laney spotted the monster whitetail twice during Indiana's 2000 archery season. On opening day of gun season, Laney and his son, Rick, again spotted the monarch, but the deer eluded them. When the season ended, there had been no reports of bagging the buck, and the Laneys hoped the deer survived.

The Laney family has a passion for shed hunting, finding about 20 sheds every year. In February 2001 Kyle found a nice 4-point shed. He and his wife, Patty, searched for the matching half, but to no avail. However, the match was quickly forgotten when Patty screamed that she had found the 5-point shed from the huge buck Kyle and Rick had seen.

The Laneys began a quest to find the matching 5-point shed, which lasted several evenings. Then, one night on the way home, Kyle found the mate behind a brush pile 100 yards from where Patty had found the first shed. This invigorated the Laneys as they anticipated the fall 2001 hunting season.

During bow season, Rick found huge scrapes and rubs on the ridge where he hunted and was confident the big buck was in the area, but the giant never showed.

Thick fog greeted the Laneys on opening morning of gun season, making hunting nearly impossible. Disappointed by the morning hunt, the Laney clan assembled for lunch at home. However, when they got there, Rick was missing.

Rick's step-brother had set up closest to Rick, and had heard a single shot from Rick's direction.

Kyle and his son, Brian, decided to check on Rick. When they got to Rick's stand, Rick was sitting next to the giant whitetail. Rick was so excited, he wouldn't leave the deer!

The buck passed Rick's stand at 9:30, and Rick shook so much he had to kneel to steady himself in his climbing tree stand, but one shot from his Remington 870 dropped the buck. Rick knew it was the monster and he shook so much he could hardly descend from his tree stand.

The 9-pointer measured 152 inches and weighed 195 pounds.

Mother, Daughter Experience Success

HUNTER: **Tanya Schroeder**
DATE: **Nov. 23, 2002**
LOCATION: **Wisconsin**
METHOD: **7mm08 Rifle**
RACK: **8-point buck**

Opening day of Wisconsin's 2002 gun-deer season was a memorable one for the Schroeder family of Shawano, Wis.

On opening morning, 14-year-old Tanya was hunting with her father, Lowell. At about 6:30 a.m., Lowell saw a large deer, but it was too dark to tell what it was. Lowell and Tanya watched the deer for about 15 minutes, then it started running in circles with its nose to the ground. Lowell knew it had to be a buck trying to pick up the scent of does that passed through earlier. Seconds later, they saw the buck's antlers.

Tanya decided to shoot the bruiser. She shouldered her 7mm08, put the cross hairs behind the buck's shoulder and fired. The buck dropped in its tracks.

Tanya's 8-pointer had an $18\frac{1}{2}$-inch spread and field dressed at 180 pounds.

Meanwhile, Tanya's mother, Cindy, was hunting nearby. Cindy had began hunting two years earlier, taking hunter's safety with her daughter and catching the same hunting bug Tanya had.

HUNTER: **Cindy Schroeder**
DATE: **Nov. 23, 2002**
LOCATION: **Wisconsin**
METHOD: **Gun**
RACK: **6-point buck**

Cindy heard her daughter shoot at 6:45 a.m. About a half-hour later, it was her turn. A lone deer sneaked through the brush. As it came closer, she saw that it was a buck. When it was 60 yards away, she fired. The 6-pointer was her first buck, and although she was excited, she was even more excited to see Tanya's buck!

Huge Rubs Lead Virginia Hunter to Buck

Bruce Lewis of Fredericksburg, Va., works hard for his bucks. Lewis and his friends and relatives hunt from a cabin deep in the George Washington National Forest. Deer sightings are few, but the chance of tagging a true Big Woods trophy is incentive enough to keep them going.

In 2001, as usual, most hunters in camp left the day before Thanksgiving to be with their families. Lewis' family, at least partially, was already in deer camp. Lewis continued to hunt, along with his father, Jack; brother, Kent and friend Mike Shavis.

HUNTER: **Bruce Lewis**
DATE: **Nov. 22, 2001**
LOCATION: **Virginia**
METHOD: **Gun**
RACK: **12-point buck**

Lewis had hunted all day for three consecutive days without seeing a deer. However, he saw several big rubs, and he knew large bucks were out there somewhere.

Thanksgiving morning, Lewis decided to sleep in and have a big breakfast after hunting so hard for so long. The plan was for he and Shavis to make a small push on a laurel-covered ridge, where Lewis' father and brother would be waiting.

After a mile-long walk from the cabin, Lewis and Shavis reached the starting point at 8 a.m. They were just about to discuss strategy when Lewis heard something moving to his right.

He and Shavis readied themselves, and a shot rang out close by. A doe popped out of the woods, running at full-tilt. Behind the doe was a big buck.

Lewis raised his rifle and fired. The bullet struck the buck in the spine and dropped it. A follow-up shot killed the buck quickly.

Only when the buck hit the ground did Lewis realize how big its rack was.

Lewis and his hunting partners assembled around the fallen 12-pointer, and when Lewis got a good, up-close look at largest buck he'd ever killed, all the long, uneventful hours he'd spent hunting suddenly seemed very worthwhile.

Shooting his best buck deep in the forest and in the company of family and a close friend helped Lewis realize he truly has a lot to be thankful for.

Father and Son Find New Spot, Relationship

My father, Dick Pamer, and I had been planning our annual Ohio deer hunt since the last day of spring turkey season. We had hunted the same private property for the past several years, and we had a good idea of deer patterns. We filled our tags in each of the last four seasons, and we were confident this year would be no different. Excitement grew as we mapped out our strategy and stand locations on the land we knew so well. Then the worst happened: the landowner sold his land. I felt as though the gift that I had wanted for 10 years was ripped from my hands as I opened it on Christmas morning.

HUNTER: **Kevin Pamer**
DATE: **November 2002**
LOCATION: **Ohio**
METHOD: **Bow**
RACK: **14-point buck, 170-class**

With two weeks between the bad news and our hunt, and no permission to hunt private property, there was the possibility that our deer season may not exist. Sure, we could probably find a spot to hunt on public land, but that never interested us. About a week before our vacation, my dad received permission from a farmer to hunt his property approximately one hour from our homes. With very little time to scout the land, we accepted the fact that this season would be a blind adventure. Although I didn't get a chance to scout, my dad walked the property one morning before work.

Our hunt started on Nov. 11. As we approached the unfamiliar timber that we would call home for the next week, I couldn't help but feel apprehensive.

My dad had found a few large rubs along the field's edge and the woods the week before, and decided that would be a good place to start. We walked together in total darkness to the field's edge and decided that a large ash tree would be as good a place as any to hang a stand. As I began climbing, dad vanished into the darkness on his way to his stand site about 200 yards from mine. Dad chose a well-used trail about 80 yards inside the woods to set up his ambush.

As the sun began to show its first signs of daylight, I looked around at my new surroundings. Off in the distance I noticed a deer working along the field's edge. It was a buck, and it was heading my way.

At about 80 yards, it turned and entered the safety of the woods. In no time, I could make out some movement through the thick cover below me. It was the buck. It was only a 6-pointer, but it was coming right to me. As it approached bow-range, the cover became thicker and I had no shot. As the buck walked by, and it grew lighter, I could see that I had no shooting lanes from this location. I knew at this point I had to move my stand.

At 11:30 a.m., I called my dad on his cell phone to check in and hear if he had any luck. He said that he watched a mature buck that had moved to within 100 yards of his stand and bedded down. He thought at first the big buck was shot, as it seemed lethargic and kept dropping its head. Then suddenly the bruiser stood and took a few steps. In front of him lay a doe it had been trying to breed. The doe arose from its bed, moved about 10 yards, then bedded down again.

My dad said, "He's tall and wide and looks like a reindeer."

Because stalking the buck was out of the question, due to the crisp fall leaves and wind direction, Dad decided to stay in his tree until dark in hopes that the doe would use the trail to lure the bruiser past him. With not an ounce of daylight left in the day, dad quietly climbed down to the ground, knowing the doe and buck remained not 100 yards away in the darkness.

Back at camp there was talk of the day's activities, including three does and the small buck I had seen, but nothing had us more excited than knowing a trophy buck was living in the woods we received permission to hunt not two weeks earlier.

The next morning the 5:30 a.m., alarm stirred us to life in our camper. Day 2 of our hunt on this unfamiliar ground had new meaning as the anticipation of the big buck's whereabouts kept our adrenaline flowing. As we parted ways to our respective stands, a simple "good luck" was all that was needed to instill new hope for the day's hunt.

As the sun rose, a doe and its yearling ambled through the trees below me not 20 yards away. With still no shot due to the heavy cover, I decided that today I had to move my stand. At noon dad called and said he was heading back to camp to warm up and get a bite to eat. I decided it was time to relocate my stand and join dad for lunch.

I moved about 40 yards deeper into the woods and set up on two converging trails. From this vantage point, I had several shooting lanes and I felt confident that deer moved through here frequently.

After eating lunch and discussing the morning's events, we headed back out for our evening hunt. With neither of us seeing the bruiser that morning, we hoped it would make an appearance that evening.

After climbing back into my new tree, I began to pick out shooting lanes, and with the aid of my laser range-finder, found distances to landmarks so I could make an accurate shot.

From my new location I noticed that I still had an opening to shoot through out into the open field if a deer took that route. It would be a 40-yard shot, but I thought I could make it.

As daylight slowly slipped away, I caught some movement along the edge of the field and the woods. I didn't need a second glance, as I knew this must be the bruiser my dad watched with a doe the day before. Indeed it was tall and wide, just as my dad described him. As it moved along the edge, I hoped it would turn down one of the two trails leading to my stand, offering me a 10-yard shot. When it walked past the trails, I knew my only shot would be the 40-yarder I previously gauged with my range-finder.

The buck moved along, testing the air for any signs of danger or an estrous doe. When it was 5 yards from my shot opening, I came to full draw. As it stepped into my window, I stopped the buck with a bleat and let the arrow fly. Five minutes passed as I gathered my wits and called my dad to let him know I had taken a shot at his "reindeer."

By the time my feet were on solid ground, it was already dark enough to use my flashlight. I searched the area where it stood and found no blood or my arrow. I wasn't sure where I had hit it, or if I had hit it at all because it was fairly dark when I made the shot. As I walked in the direction the buck fled, my light reflected off the nock of my arrow about 60 yards from where the deer stood when I shot. The arrow was covered with blood. Dad met me in the field and we decided it was too dark to make a recovery that night, not knowing where the deer was hit.

The night of Nov. 12, found me lying awake, wondering if we would find the buck. We agreed to hunt the morning hours before searching for the trophy, but at 8:30 a.m., I couldn't take it anymore and called dad to let him know I was starting the search. I think, even though my dad didn't shoot the buck, he was just as excited as I was to find it.

After trailing the buck with very little blood to follow, due to a light mist during the night, we found where it jumped a fence and reentered the woods. All the while, dad kept telling me "You've got him; we'll find him," even when the trail seemed to end at times.

After we crossed the fence, my dad said, "There he is," and sure enough, there it was about 50 yards inside the woods.

After sharing a congratulatory hug and some high fives, I realized something, that deep inside, I had known all along.

Hunting with my father is something I wouldn't trade for anything, and I hope it means as much to my 6-year-old son, Trey, some day as it means to me. After all, hunting with my father means more than the trophy to me.

— Kevin Pamer

Father Beats Cancer, Sees Son Bag First Buck

Tim Cowles of Franconia, N.H., is a whitetail fanatic. He has enjoyed deer hunting for 25 years and has killed several nice deer. But none are as memorable as the one his son, Tucker, shot in November 2002.

In October 2001, Tim Cowles was diagnosed with cancer and was given a 50 percent chance to live. He underwent radiation, surgery and chemotherapy, which tortured him physically and mentally.

However, after a year of battling his cancer, he gathered enough strength to take Tucker hunting.

HUNTER: **Tucker Cowles**
DATE: **Nov. 24, 2002**
LOCATION: **New Hampshire**
METHOD: **.357 Mag.**
RACK: **8-point buck**

It was Tucker's fourth season, and he had never shot a deer. The Cowles hunted with a friend, Duane Cross, who knew an area that a spike buck frequented. He would also serve as videographer for Tucker's hunt on Nov. 24, 2002.

That morning dawned cold and windy. Six inches of new-fallen snow blanketed the clear-cut the hunters headed for.

The spike did not appear, and after several uneventful hours, the crew was cold and was about ready to leave when a nice buck poked its head out of the red maple whips.

The buck was screened by the dense, regenerating maples and didn't offer a shot. The elder Cowles was impressed with his son's patience as they waited and hoped the buck would draw nearer.

After 8 minutes, the buck came to within 100 yards and gave Tucker the broadside shot he'd been hoping for. His .357 Mag. barked and the buck jumped into the air, then sped off in a death run.

Cowles admired his son's patience, concentration and gun-handling, especially in the excitement following the shot. He could tell that even if he'd have lost his battle with cancer, he'd done a good job raising his son, and he was proud of him.

The hunters followed a short blood trail to the heart-shot 8-pointer, which carried a 19½-inch spread.

LEONARD DIDONATO killed this big Saskatchewan 8-pointer during the last hour of his Canadian hunt. It is the largest he's killed in more than a half-century of deer hunting.

6

Antlers Across America

N.J. Hunter Kills 11th-Hour Whitetail

Leonard Didonato of Princeton, N.J., celebrated his 72nd birthday, but his sons got the present.

Didonato has hunted whitetails for 55 years in numerous states and in Canada. For his birthday in 2002, he took his sons with him on a Saskatchewan deer hunt.

Didonato saw several deer during his week-long hunt, and four of the six hunters in camp had killed nice bucks, but on the last morning of the hunt, Didonato's tag remained unfilled.

On Nov. 11, Didonato only had until noon to hunt before packing up and heading for home. A foot of snow lay on the ground and the trees were covered like a winter wonderland. It was a picturesque setting for his last morning of hunting, if nothing else.

Didonato had used his grunt tube several times that morning with no success. With time running out and nothing to lose, at 11:00, he produced one final grunt.

Five minutes later, a big 8-pointer appeared over Didonato's left shoulder.

Didonato let the buck walk past him, as he was out of position for a shot. Didonato carefully reached for his 7 mm as the buck passed, but the scope pinged on the ice-covered tree stand.

The buck spun around and looked right at Didonato, then bolted toward the thick Canadian bush.

Didonato knew he had little time to shoot before the buck disappeared. He shouldered the rifle, swung hard and pulled the trigger.

The bullet nailed the big 8-pointer in the spine, and the buck slid to the ground. Didonato finished it with a quick follow-up shot.

The 8-pointer grossed 136 inches and its longest tine is 12 1/8 inches. The buck weighed 287 pounds.

The dramatic last-second buck was a special birthday present for Didonato, because it is the largest he's killed in more than a half-century of deer hunting. And he killed it on the 11th hour of the 11th day of the 11th month.

Busy Contractor Finds Time to Bag His Buck

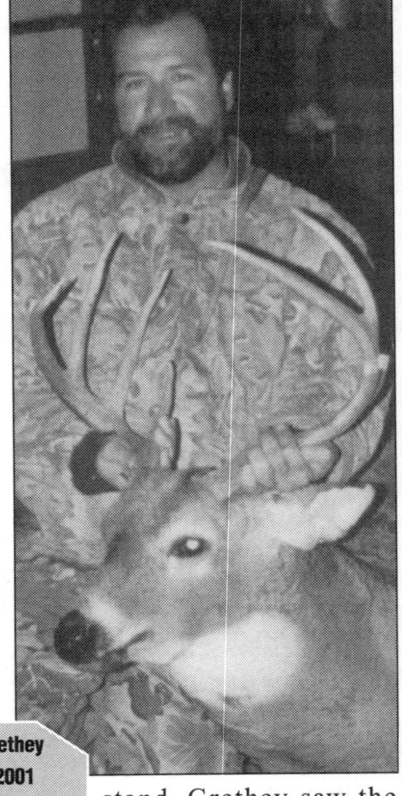

Victor Grethey, like a lot of people, is too busy to hunt very often. A general contractor by trade, Grethey works from 6 a.m. to 9 p.m.

Grethey's wife, Lisa, bought him a bow for Christmas one year because he never takes time for himself. She hoped the new bow would give him incentive to get into the woods more often. She knows her husband is really at peace when there is no phone and no one to bother him while he bow-hunts.

In October of 2001, Grethey found some time to hunt, sitting in the same tree stand next to a standing cornfield for eight consecutive days.

The eighth hunt proved to be a memorable one.

HUNTER: **Victor Grethey**
DATE: **October 2001**
LOCATION: **Illinois**
METHOD: **Bow**
RACK: **7-point buck**

Grethey saw a high-racked buck walking about 400 yards behind him. The buck was heading diagonally in Grethey's direction.

When the buck approached to 60 yards, it turned parallel to Grethey, then proceeded to a waterway 20 yards to Grethey's right.

When the buck stood 25 yards away, Grethey lined up his pendulum sight on the buck's vitals and released his arrow. Grethey knew he'd made a good hit.

The buck turned to its right and rocketed through the cornfield.

From his perch high in his tree stand, Grethey saw the buck's wide rack ripping down two rows of corn as it ran. Grethey watched the buck run like this for 80 yards, before it disappeared from view.

Grethey waited 35 minutes before trailing his buck. After a 10-minute tracking job that covered 100 yards, Grethey recovered his long-tined buck, which field dressed at 265 pounds!

Grethey was so excited he couldn't even talk to his wife on the phone to tell her he'd gotten a buck.

Bow Shop Owner Brings in the Trophy

Jody Mork of Iola, Wis., needs no introduction to big bucks. As owner of J.R.'s Sport Shop, the self-proclaimed bow-hunting capitol of the nation, he sees his share of monster whitetails brought to his shop. However, an accomplished bow-hunter himself, he's tagged a few trophies as well.

The 2002 archery season looked promising for Mork. Mork hunts on leased land in a quality deer management program. His friend's farm borders this land, and he, too practices QDM. In summer 2002, Mork saw a bachelor group of four 2½-year-old bucks, along with a 4½-year-old, 13-point monster.

HUNTER: **Jody Mork**
DATE: **Oct. 16, 2002**
LOCATION: **Wisconsin**
METHOD: **Bow**
RACK: **13-point buck**

During archery season, Mork saw the 13-pointer just about every week while scouting in the evenings from his truck. Mork had a good idea where the buck bedded, but he needed a north wind to hunt the trophy buck. However, in early fall of 2002, north winds were few.

When Mork finally got a north wind, he set up near the buck's bedding area on the peak of a ridge with a small area of brushy pines.

The first hunt was fruitless, and so was his second hunt with a north wind. Mork had moved closer to the buck's bedding area on the second hunt, so when he entered the woods on Oct. 16, he set up even closer to the bedding area.

It was clear and about 25 degrees. Mork set up near a fork in two logging roads.

Mork was watching four does and fawns when he noticed the 13-pointer on the logging road. The buck had slipped in quietly and was only 10 yards away when Mork first saw it. Mork never stood up. He waited until the buck's head was behind a tree and drew. When the buck presented a shot, Mork released. The mortally wounded buck ran right under Mork's stand, ran about 35 yards, and expired.

The 13-pointer sported a tall, forked brow tine with a third point on its left side. This unusual rack characteristic could be explained by an injury to the buck's right hind leg, which was about 2 inches shorter than the left and sported a baseball-sized calcium growth.

Mork's buck grossed 160 inches and dressed at 222 pounds.

Michigan Hunter Has November to Remember

For a few days in November 1998, Jerry Paauwe of Grand Rapids, Mich., must have felt like a deer hunting superstar.

On Nov. 4, Paauwe was sitting 20 feet up a white pine as morning broke. He had placed his stand a week earlier near a bedding area, and since then, a scrape and some rubs had appeared.

While he sat that frosty morning, he thought he saw steam in the brush. Then a large set of antlers emerged. The buck was headed for the scrape, which was 20 yards away. Paauwe prepared for an easy shot.

HUNTER: **Jerry Paauwe**
DATE: **Nov. 4, 8, 1998**
LOCATION: **Michigan**
METHOD: **Bow**
RACK: **8-point bucks**

Things didn't quite go as planned. The buck walked through the scrape and continued head-on toward Paauwe, and soon stood directly below him! Branches prevented Paauwe from seeing the buck. All he could do was hope the deer wouldn't spook.

Finally, the buck walked back toward the scrape. When it turned slightly, Paauwe launched his arrow and the buck took off.

When Paauwe climbed down from his stand, he noticed a fresh rub on a pine sapling below him. He approached the scrape and found a good blood trail. He called home for his sons, but they weren't home, so his wife had to help him drag his buck.

Paauwe's luck continued on Nov. 8. Paauwe went to a different area where he knew does and fawns bedded. He noticed increased buck sign in the area and hung a stand in a maple tree near two trails. At 4 p.m. Paauwe went back to his new stand. At 5:40 p.m. Paauwe heard a twig snap and spotted a nice buck that was bigger than the one he'd shot four days earlier.

Paauwe was not allowed to trim branches in this hunting area, so when he set up, he intended to face the tree when he shot. Now he struggle do twist his body into shooting position, and soon the buck would be downwind of him. As Paauwe came to full draw, he had to hold a limb out of his way. The buck was quartering away when Paauwe released his arrow. Paauwe's shot was true and with the help of his son, Jim, Paauwe recovered his second big buck in less than a week!

Buck No. 57 As Exciting As First Spike in 1964

Norman Dann of Peterboro, N.Y., has a certain familiarity with a 1,000-acre cedar swamp in central New York. The swamp is so large, diverse and stable that few venture into it. Dann says the deer know it, and feel safe there, and that's why Dann says if mankind vanished tomorrow, the swamp would never know it.

Well, it might.

Dann's presence there is almost as common as the deer he hunts there. Between "Old Faithful" — one of his deer stands in the swamp — and two nearby stands, Dann has killed 30 bucks in the swamp. His most recent he killed Nov. 24, 2002.

HUNTER: **Norman Dann**
DATE: **Nov. 24, 2002**
LOCATION: **New York**
METHOD: **Gun**
RACK: **7-point buck**

By that time, the hills surrounding the swamps had been pounded by hunters for nearly a week, making his "Brook Corner" stand in the middle of the swamp an ideal place to intercept deer seeking refuge from intruding hunters. Dann had spotted a large solitary track in the early snowfall and fantasized that a wise, old swamp buck left the track.

Dann donned high rubber boots to get to his stand away from the crowds deep in the wet swamp.

The day dawned clear and cold with several inches of fresh snow, which limited visibility.

Dann passed the first two hours on stand watching a mink hunt along the edge of a brook.

At 8:30, Dann spotted movement behind the thick cedars 30 yards to the north. At first he thought it was the mink he was watching, but when he saw brown fur, he thought it was a coyote. However, when the buck poked its head out from behind the cedars, looking for a place to cross the brook, there was no mistaking the buck's antlers.

The buck was screened by cedars as it looked for a good crossing, all the while drawing closer before Dann fired his killing shot.

It took Dann two hours to float the buck out of the swamp back to the truck, and even though this was the 57th buck Dann has killed, he said shooting it was every bit as exciting as shooting his first deer — a spike buck — in 1964.

The 2½-year-old 7-pointer had a 15-inch inside spread and field dressed at 187 pounds.

Hunter Seeks Buck But Finds Redemption

Scott Barkley of Fulton, N.J. didn't go to his deer stand on opening morning of New Jersey's 1998 gun season for redemption. He went to bag one of the three small bucks he'd seen that had eluded him during the bow season.

That morning, Barkley carried his shotgun into the stand where he'd bow-hunted earlier in the year. At about 8 a.m., he saw a doe with a 6-pointer trailing her. The deer were heading toward Barkley's stand.

HUNTER: **Scott Barkley**
DATE: **Opening Day 1998**
LOCATION: **New Jersey**
METHOD: **Gun**
RACK: **8-point buck**

As Barkley watched the deer stroll closer to his stand though his scope, he saw the doe freeze and the 6-pointer take off on a tear.

Off to his left, Barkley caught movement and slowly turned in that direction. A nice buck was sneaking toward the doe, grunting all the way.

The doe was now centered in one of Barkley's shooting lanes about 35 yards away. While Barkley struggled to find an opening in which to shoot the buck, he couldn't help but notice the size of the buck's antlers. The buck was bigger than any he'd ever shot before.

As Barkley switched the safety off, the buck strolled up behind the doe and right into Barkley's shooting lane. Barkley steadied the cross hairs on the buck's left shoulder the best he could in his excitement and slowly squeezed the trigger.

The buck dropped, got back up, and stumbled 20 yards before crashing down for good within sight of Barkley's stand.

Looking back on the hunt, Barkley realized that it had an air of redemption. After all the times Barkley had cursed does for seeing him, smelling him or somehow sensing that he was there and blowing his hunt, things had come full circle.

In fact, Barkley reasons the doe he saw that morning had probably ruined his hunt before, but that morning it was responsible for Barkley getting a shot at his biggest buck ever. Sometimes things have a way of working out.

Barkley's 8-pointer had a 19½-inch inside spread and tipped the scales at 190 pounds. The buck was 4½ years old.

Travis Hall
South Texas
160-class buck

Daniel E. Schmidt

Canceled Appointment Leads to 11-Pointer

Tim Gargana of Rochester, N.Y., felt the crunch in the fall of 2002. As a mortgage banker, he was flooded with calls from his clients as interest rates kept dropping. But on Nov. 11, his afternoon appointment canceled, and he had to make a decision: stay at work and catch up on paperwork or go bow-hunting.

It was an easy decision, and soon Gargana was headed to a friend's property. The friend has a $300,000 house with a 2-acre yard, surrounded by 17 acres of scrub trees. Deer frequent the area, so Gargana headed for his $40 tree stand to ponder the ironies of suburban hunting.

HUNTER: **Tim Gargana**
DATE: **Nov. 11, 2002**
LOCATION: **New York**
METHOD: **Bow**
RACK: **11-point buck**

After about 2 hours, Gargana had seen a fox, a cat and ducks and geese, but not a single deer. With 15 minutes of shooting light left, he unsnapped his fanny pack and started to organize things for his descent when he heard a deer coming. He snapped his fanny pack back on and grabbed his bow.

A nice buck stepped out of a hedgerow and walked 10 yards behind Gargana.

At this point Gargana was just pleased to see the deer, which gave him confidence for his next hunt, but it wasn't over. Sensing something wasn't right, the buck circled Gargana's tree. Gargana grunted when the buck was 18 yards away, stopping the buck. Gargana shot and the buck crashed away into the brush.

Gargana called his wife, and he could hear his son yelling excitedly in the background. He also called his two brothers, and soon all four people met him at his tree stand to help trail the buck.

Gargana felt confident in his shot and thought he heard the buck fall, but everything became a blur in the excitement of the moment.

But his observations were right on. They found a good blood trail, and his double-lung shot dropped the buck after it traveled 70 yards.

The 11-pointer had split brow tines and field dressed at 218 pounds.

Velvet Buck is a Surprise

HUNTER: **Richard Claire**
DATE: **Nov. 1, 2000**
LOCATION: **Missouri**
METHOD: **Bow**
RACK: **10-point buck**

Richard Claire of Greenwood, Mo., tries to take vacation during the last few days of October and first few days of November so he can bow-hunt. During his week off in 2000, deer activity had increased, but as the week wound down, he still hadn't tagged a buck. On Halloween, Claire passed on a small 10-pointer, and now as the week faded and gun season drew closer, he reconsidered his decision and decided to shoot if he saw the deer again.

Claire was optimistic when he climbed into his stand Nov. 1. He had seen an 8-pointer in addition to the 10-pointer the day before, and both bucks had appeared by 8:30. But when 10 a.m. rolled around on this morning, he still hadn't seen a deer. He decided to hunt for another half-hour, and then call it quits.

Suddenly, Claire heard hoofs pounding on the ground close by. The deer was running away from his blind. Then the deer stopped, whirled and started to walk toward the blind, apparently catching a whiff of the estrous-doe scent Claire had placed in the area.

Claire picked up his bow and got ready for a shot. Claire new the buck had a nice rack, but there was something unusual about it. Claire thought perhaps it was a nontypical, and because he'd never shot a buck with an abnormal rack, he grew excited. But by the time he drew and sighted, the buck was quartering away and getting on the far edge of his effective range.

Claire hurried his shot, and made the hit of a lifetime. His errant arrow struck the deer between the ear and the eye, and the deer dropped without flinching.

When Claire got out of his blind, he saw a 6-pointer standing where the buck had stood. Claire thought he'd overestimated the size of the buck, and prepared for a finishing shot on the deer when he noticed tines on the ground. The 6-pointer was a different buck.

Claire got another surprise when he gutted the velvet-antlered 10-pointer. The deer had no testicles! This is probably the reason why the antlers were still in velvet.

Does Tip-Off Hunter To Good Buck Location

While heading deep into the woods for a mid-November hunt, John Van Heynigen of Chester, Mass., spotted two does in a secluded field.

He paused to watch them eat, then disappear into a hardwood sidehill.

The rut was gearing up, and Van Heynigen decided it might be a good idea to hunt where he'd seen the two does. He'd scouted the area a few days before and had found several fresh scrapes and rubs near the field edge.

HUNTER: **John Van Heynigen**
DATE: **November 2002**
LOCATION: **Massachusetts**
METHOD: **Bow**
RACK: **9-point buck**

Although he didn't see any more deer that afternoon, he left his climbing stand at the base of his tree, as he planned to return in the morning.

The next morning, after climbing the tree, he realized he'd forgotten to hang his scent canister. Rather than climb down, he opened his bottle of dominant tarsal scent and squirted it onto the ground. Even 28 feet in the air, he could smell the strong odor.

At 8 a.m., he picked up is grunt call and made a few long, low, guttural grunts, followed by some short tending grunts.

He'd barely finished the sequence when he heard leaves crunching. A buck was approaching to investigate the "intruder" buck. As soon as Van Heynigen saw the buck, he knew it was a shooter.

The buck was about 70 yards away, with its head low to the ground. It started to turn back in the direction from which it had came, but Van Heynigen snapped up the grunt call and gave one more low grunt. The buck froze and looked back in Van Heynigen's direction, then hustled toward him.

The buck closed the distance quickly and soon was almost directly below Van Heynigen, but Van Heynigen's quiver hit his stand's seat bar, and he couldn't shoot.

The buck walked behind Van Heynigen, giving the hunter a chance to reposition for a shot. When the buck was 15 yards behind him, Van Heynigen released his arrow. The 9-pointer ran about 100 yards before expiring.

Hunter Learns to Always Carry Your Bow

Earl Travis of Paw Paw, W.Va., has had few encounters with big bucks. And the times he has seen them, they've been running or out of bow range. The only chance he ever had at a nice buck was when as an excited teenager, he shot over the back of a nice buck.

Travis finally got another good chance on opening day of West Virginia's 2002 archery season. Armed with a new tree stand and new arrows, Travis was in his favorite tree before daylight.

HUNTER: **Earl Travis (right)**
DATE: **Opening Day 2002**
LOCATION: **West Virginia**
METHOD: **Bow**
RACK: **7-point buck**

A doe and fawn emerged early, and had it been later in the season, Travis would have shot, but it was opening morning, so he waited.

At 8:55, he saw three deer to his right, and the last one was a nice buck. Travis' heart pounded double time as he drew his bow and waited for his chance. The first two deer slowly passed his position. The buck was on a course that would lead past Travis' stand at 30 yards.

Travis' arms ached as he held the bow. "What if the deer smells me or hears me breathing," he thought.

Finally, the buck stepped in the opening and Travis shot, hitting the buck high in the shoulder. The buck dropped and rolled down the mountain. For a moment Travis heard the buck thrashing below, then there was silence.

Travis didn't want to ruin the hunt for his partner, Tim Landis, so he waited a while. Finally, he could stand it no longer and met Landis at his stand.

Travis explained the situation, and they left their gear at the truck. Landis suggested Travis should leave his bow behind so dragging the deer would be easier.

When the hunters followed the trail, they found the buck, but it was still alive. Travis' heart raced. He didn't want to lose that deer!

Landis kept an eye on the buck while Travis went back to the truck for his bow. After a well-placed shot, Travis tagged his best buck ever!

Peter Whitaker
Western Missouri, November 1999
3-beamed buck

Daniel E. Schmidt

Bow-Hunter Tags Buck In Whitetail Paradise

Lee Lancaster of Snellville, Ga., traveled to famous Pike County, Ill., with his three hunting partners. The quartet had hunted together in Georgia for years, but this was their first out-of-state hunt.

The first day Lancaster saw an 8-pointer and a 10-pointer chasing a doe right under his stand, but neither was big enough to shoot. He saw the same deer again later that day, as well as a wide-racked 6-pointer that chased three does. Before the day was over, Lancaster had spotted five more does, a 4-pointer, another 8-pointer and another 10-pointer.

HUNTER: **Lee Lancaster**
DATE: **2002**
LOCATION: **Illinois**
METHOD: **Bow**
RACK: **9-point buck**

Lancaster couldn't believe how good the hunting had been. He had plenty to look forward to on Day 2.

The second morning Lancaster saw several of the same deer again, so he decided to move for his afternoon hunt.

In the afternoon, five does fed in front of him on a classic, picturesque fall day. As daylight faded, a pair of 8-pointers entered the field, chasing a doe. Again, however, they weren't big enough for Lancaster.

Back at camp, his friend, Rick, had bagged a nice 10-pointer.

The third day Lancaster hunted in a draw at the intersection of two fields. A spike fed along the edge of one field, and as it eased closer, it suddenly came to full alert. Four does stepped into the field, followed by a nice 10-pointer. The deer never got close enough for a shot, despite the grunts Lancaster produced on his grunt tube.

The fourth morning Lancaster reflected on his hunt. He had seen so many deer and had so much fun that even if he didn't get a deer in his two remaining days, the hunt had been well worth it.

A snapping twig downhill and to his left grabbed Lancaster's attention. Soon he saw a tall-tined 9-pointer walking toward him. It was heading right for his tree.

Lancaster has never been a fan of the straight-down shot, but when the buck walked underneath him, he took it and connected.

The 9-pointer ran 60 yards before crashing.

Hunter Follows Instincts To Nice 10-Point Buck

Sometimes a nagging feeling can be so overpowering that it overwhelms you. Roy Schneiderman of Lancaster, N.Y. found this out on Nov. 8, 2002.

It was an unseasonably warm day for November in New York, but the timing was right for rutting activity. Schneiderman rushed to complete his chores so he could reach his cabin in time for an afternoon bow-hunt.

HUNTER: **Roy Schneiderman**
DATE: **Nov. 8, 2002**
LOCATION: **New York**
METHOD: **Bow**
RACK: **10-point buck**

Schneiderman's hunting partners decided not to hunt that evening, due to strong southwest winds. Schneiderman struggled to decide whether to hunt a funnel on his property or a stand on a friend's farm.

Schneiderman decided to hunt on his friend's land, but as he climbed into his tree stand, a strong feeling came over him. He felt like he should have gone to his other stand. The feeling grew in intensity, and after about an hour, he climbed down and trotted to his truck, bound for the other stand.

After reaching the cabin, parking, and racing to his stand, he only had a half-hour of shooting light left. Schneiderman began to feel stupid. He had ran around in the woods, hopping from stand to stand, and now the hunt was almost over. He tried to make something happen.

Schneiderman made three doe bleats on his call. Then he reflected on the bucks he'd passed up, fearing he wouldn't get another chance.

Just then he noticed movement. A set of antlers appeared first, and Schneiderman saw that a nice buck was heading his way.

Schneiderman took his eyes off the rack to concentrate on shooting. The buck passed through his first shooting lane, and for some reason, Schneiderman didn't shoot. When the buck was 8 yards away, Schneiderman shot.

With daylight fading, Schneiderman climbed down and returned to the cabin to enlist the help of his hunting partners in finding the buck.

They recovered the 245-pound 10-pointer 120 yards into the swamp.

Ohio Man Shoots Buck From Old Kitchen Chair

While everyone knows bagging a trophy buck usually takes a tremendous amount of skill, sometimes all it takes is a little luck and an old kitchen chair.

Ed Meister of Brooklyn, Ohio, and his friend, George, traveled to their hunting camp in preparation for Ohio's 2001 shotgun season. After meeting their friend, Bob, they sighted in their guns.

HUNTER: **Ed Meister**
DATE: **Opening Day 2001**
LOCATION: **Ohio**
METHOD: **Shotgun**
RACK: **11-point buck**

George and Bob tote nice guns with scopes and rifled barrels, but Meister uses a cheap, old 20-gauge side-by-side. Meister's first shot completely missed the target, as did the second. He tried the other barrel, and he was accurate. So now he knew he was limited to one shot out of the left barrel.

Meister planned to sit along a creek on opening morning, so George, placed an old kitchen chair there for him.

Opening morning Meister found the chair in the dark, then settled down and waited.

Right away he heard a pair of shots nearby, then a few more shots in the distance, then all was quiet.

Minutes later Meister detected movement, and when he turned his eyes, he saw the biggest buck he'd ever seen!

The buck was trotting in his direction. Meister placed his shotgun's bead behind the front shoulder and pulled the trigger, but nothing happened. He pulled the wrong trigger!

The buck passed Meister, and when it stopped after crossing the creek, Meister pulled the left trigger, and the buck flipped backward down the ditch bank and struggled to get up. Meister tried top break open his shotgun, but it was jammed. He broke it open across his knee, but by then the buck was still.

Meister's buck was so big he needed help field dressing and moving it.

Meister couldn't believe his luck. Not only had he shot his biggest buck ever, it fell next to a creek, which made washing after field dressing a snap. Plus, he'd shot it from a kitchen chair right in the open!

Michigan Man Tags Buck On a Hunch

John Eggenberger, of Ypsilanti, Mich., has had hunches before, but never one like the one he had Nov. 22, 1998.

Eggenberger hunts state land in southeastern Michigan. These areas receive heavy hunting pressure, so Eggenberger seeks out thick swamps "where no normal human would want to go."

During bow-season, he frequently hunted from one of his favorite stands, but unlike in past years, he only saw one deer all season, despite plentiful deer sign.

HUNTER: **John Eggenberger**
DATE: **Nov. 22, 1998**
LOCATION: **Michigan**
METHOD: **Gun**
RACK: **8-point buck**

As gun-season approached, he thought about looking for a better spot, but something told him to stay put. On opening morning of gun-season, he shot a large doe that approached to within 20 yards.

A week later Eggenberger was thinking about moving his stand again. Again, something told him not to move it. Besides, from his position, he could see out into an open field. It was one of the few places in the tamarack swamp where he could see more than a few yards.

Around 8:20 that morning, Eggenberger had a strong feeling about how his day would unfold. He envisioned that at 10:50 a.m., a buck with 4 points on the left and 3 on the right would come from the thicket and into the open 65 yards away.

Eggenberger had experienced thoughts like this, but never so powerful. And every time he'd ever had this sort of vision, it had come true. Eggenberger sat back, confident that the morning would unfold just as he'd envisioned.

Well, it didn't. Not quite anyway.

The buck appeared a little early — at 8:40. However, it showed up right where Eggenberger expected it to.

Eggenberger tried to whistle, but his cold, quivering lips only produced a hiss. Still, the buck stopped, and Eggenberger dropped it.

When he recovered the buck, he found his buck was an 8-pointer, and not a 7-pointer as he'd envisioned.

South Carolina Man Shows Up Younger Men

Bernard Stubbs of Cheraw, S.C., was one of 30 hunters who drew a tag for a hunt at Donnelly Wildlife Management Area in South Carolina.

Stubbs had suffered from vertigo earlier in the year and was equipped with a cane. He asked to be outfitted with a ground blind for his hunt, instead of one of the usual elevated stands.

Stubbs drew strange looks from the other hunters, as he was treated to the pickup's air-conditioned cab on the way to his stand.

HUNTER: **Bernard Stubbs**
DATE: **2001**
LOCATION: **South Carolina**
METHOD: **Gun**
RACK: **8-point buck**

A young man led Stubbs to his ground blind situated next to a green field. However, the bind was directly below a 10-foot ladder stand.

Stubbs gave in to temptation and climbed into the ladder stand. It took him a while, but with a little patience, he made it into the stand at 2:30 p.m.

It was 80 degrees out, and Stubbs was sweating. What's worse, the wind was blowing his scent into the green field. Stubbs removed his shirt, but then no-see-ums plagued him relentlessly.

Finally, at about 4 p.m., the sun went behind some trees and the wind shifted. Things were looking up. Stubbs relaxed and drifted off to sleep.

He awoke at 6 p.m. Ten minutes later, a buck entered the green field. Stubbs scoped the deer and looked over its rack. He was allowed to shoot either a spike or a buck with at least 4 points on one side. Stubbs saw that the buck was an 8-pointer.

Stubbs slowly tightened his finger on the trigger, and the buck dropped in its tracks.

Stubbs carefully climbed down from the stand and walked to his fallen buck.

After dark when the convoy picked up Stubbs and his buck, he was the envy of all the hunters. Some even joked that they needed to start toting a cane to be successful.

Stubbs' 8-pointer weighed 180 pounds, live. It was the biggest buck shot at Donnelly Wildlife Management area in two years.

Illinois Hunter Calls Deer With His Release

Jim Scherer of Anna, Ill., couldn't see the buck, but he saw the sapling it was rubbing shaking vigorously about 70 yards away.

Scherer had already seen three small bucks that evening. It looked like this one, however, was a big boy.

Scherer grunted several times, but the buck paid him no heed. He decided to try something different.

He began scraping the head of his release against the white oak he was positioned in, trying his best to sound like another buck making a rub. Scherer hoped to show his "dominance" over the buck.

HUNTER: **Jim Scherer**
DATE: **Nov. 14, 1998**
LOCATION: **Illinois**
METHOD: **Bow**
RACK: **10-point buck**

Scherer stopped and listened intently. Now he saw sticks and leaves flying as the buck pawed the ground. Scherer gave a snort-wheeze and the buck thrashed the sapling even more vigorously.

Scherer rubbed the tree again with more intensity and gave another snort-wheeze. It was too much for the buck to handle. Scherer heard quick, steady footsteps heading for his stand.

Scherer had created a scrape 20 yards from his stand. As he peered through his binoculars, he soon saw the buck heading for the scrape.

Scherer checked his release for any obstructions. He cleaned a piece of bark out of a crevice and clipped his release to his bow-string.

When large trees restricted the buck's vision, Scherer drew and settled his pin behind the buck's front leg. When the buck stopped at the scrape, Scherer sent his arrow on its way, and although he didn't see the arrow's flight path, he knew he was right on when he touched the release.

The buck turned and ran back in the direction it had come from, but only made it 60 yards before falling.

The $3^1/_2$-year-old 10-pointer had an 18-inch spread and a mushroomed point that apparently had broken off when the antler was in velvet.

Beau Below
Northern Wisconsin, 2002
10-pointer

Doug Below

Michigan Man Loves Big Kansas Whitetails

Richard Remmert traveled to Kansas during the 2001 muzzle-loader hunt and bagged a 162-inch 8-pointer. He was so impressed with his hunt that he returned in 2002 — this time with his bow.

Remmert's outfitter asked him if he wanted a guide with him in his tree. Remmert was hesitant, but the outfitter insisted Kansas bucks come to rattling so fast that you need to be ready to shoot as soon as the rattling sequence is finished. He wasn't kidding.

HUNTER: **Richard Remmert**
DATE: **2002**
LOCATION: **Kansas**
METHOD: **Bow**
RACK: **10-point buck**

On the third evening of the hunt, Remmert and his guide, Chad, headed to their tree stand, but when they got there, the wind wasn't right and they decided to go to a different tree.

As they walked through a wheat field, they saw a large-bodied 8-pointer heading for a pond. The hunters backtracked, then crested a rise. The buck vanished.

The men hustled to their stand and climbed in. Chad rattled, but got no reaction. However, when he rattled again a short while later, a nice 10-point buck appeared.

Remmert glanced over his shoulder and saw the buck standing on a rise. Chad rattled again and the buck ran in.

The deer stayed down in a draw for a while, looking for a fight, but when it didn't find another buck, it ran off.

Chad rattled again and the buck reappeared, standing on a ridge "like he owned Kansas." A minute later, the buck charged in.

As Remmert grabbed his bow, he heard the buck stomping and grunting. However, he couldn't see the buck because he was on the opposite side of the tree.

Expecting it to be about 25 yards away, Remmert was surprised when he saw Chad pointing straight down. The buck was right below them.

Remmert waited for the buck to take a couple steps, then shot. The 140-class buck ran off, and in true Western style, rolled all the way to the bottom of a draw.

Iowa Man Ambushes Fence Line 15-Pointer

A buck sighting in the fall of 2000 helped Chris Stoneking of Muscatine, Iowa, shoot a whopper buck two years later.

On that fall 2000 day, Stoneking was bow-hunting when he spotted a huge 10-pointer that he believes would have grossed more than 200 inches. The buck was 200 yards away, and coincidentally, that day was also the last morning of Iowa's early muzzleloader season.

HUNTER: **Chris Stoneking**
DATE: **2002**
LOCATION: **Iowa**
METHOD: **Muzzleloader**
RACK: **15-point buck**

That sighting, coupled with warm weather during Iowa's recent late muzzleloader seasons prompted Stoneking to get a tag for the early season.

Stoneking enjoys shooting and regularly practiced with his muzzleloader out to 200 yards during the summer of 2002.

When muzzleloader season rolled around, Stoneking headed for a neighbor's property. Here, he had once shot a nice 8-pointer with his bow while hunting along a fence. He hoped to repeat the feat with his muzzleloader.

Stoneking had barely sat down when a yearling 8-pointer jumped the fence and began working a scrape. Suddenly a 2½-year-old 8-pointer jumped the fence and started working the same scrape. It was a nice buck, and Stoneking thought about shooting it for a moment, but he had planned to shoot a doe or a buck at least 4½ years old, and passed on the buck.

The two bucks wandered off into the field and began sparring. That's when the big boy appeared. An even larger buck jumped the fence and worked the same scrape.

Stoneking was shaking badly, and his range-finder determined the buck was 218 yards away, so he decided not to chance the shot.

Just then, the largest buck saw the lesser bucks sparring and intervened, approaching within 125 yards of Stoneking.

Stoneking collected himself and found the buck in his scope. He touched off a shot, and the 15-pointer ran 75 yards before dropping.

The buck weighed 250 pounds and green scored 175 inches.

Oral Surgeon Can't Help Odd-Racked 8-Pointer

Bill Dzyak of Boyds, Md., is an oral and maxillofacial surgeon by trade, but the buck he killed with his bow Oct. 8, 2001, needed some serious work on top of its head.

The weeks immediately following the Sept. 11, 2001, terrorist attacks were rough on Dzyak. He cancelled his New Mexico elk hunt, which was scheduled for Sept. 15, in case he was needed for hospital emergencies.

HUNTER: **Bill Dzyak**
DATE: **Oct. 8, 2001**
LOCATION: **Maryland**
METHOD: **Bow**
RACK: **8-point buck**

To deal with his anxiety over the terrorist attacks and the state of the nation, Dzyak shot his bow every day and bow-hunted every chance he could.

On Oct. 8, Dzyak sensed something unusual and exciting. It was pre-rut, and Dzyak had a good feeling about the day's hunt.

He sprayed scent on the ground 25 yards from his stand. As he climbed his tree, three presidential helicopters flew over him.

Soon after entering his stand, Dzyak spotted movement, and a 4-pointer walked underneath his stand, then ambled off into the woods. As Dzyak admired the buck, a 6-pointer emerged, following the same trail.

Dzyak hoped a bigger buck would follow.

Next came a doe. It was feeding as it plodded along. Dzyak's attention was riveted on the doe and its back trail. For a moment Dzyak thought the doe was alone, but then an odd-racked 8-pointer appeared.

Dzyak had seen this buck on prior outings but never got a shot.

The doe walked toward Dzyak's scent line, and the buck's path led it directly under Dzyak's stand as it followed the doe.

When the doe moved on, the buck followed. Dzyak drew when it was 15 yards away, and when it hesitated at 20 yards, he launched his arrow.

Dzyak's perfect shot left an easy-to-find blood trail.

When Dzyak recovered his buck, he noticed the its back left leg was injured, which may have caused the unusual antler formation.

Lucky Deer Stand Produces Two 9-Pointers

Bryan Hartney of Atlanta, Ga., hunts with his family on their property near Lomax, Ill.

In November 2002, Hartney had bow-hunted for two weeks straight. He shot a 9-pointer, but he was hoping to find something a little bigger.

Nov. 16, was the last day Hartney could hunt. It was also the first day of the Illinois shotgun season, so he traded his bow for his shotgun before heading out that morning.

HUNTER: **Bryan Hartney**
DATE: **Nov. 16, 2002**
LOCATION: **Illinois**
METHOD: **Shotgun**
RACK: **9-point buck**

After Hartney killed his 9-pointer, his fellow hunters all wanted to hunt from the stand where he'd killed it — the Hogshead Stand. However, after they hunted from the stand several times unsuccessfully, they'd given up on it.

Hartney was glad for that, and he chose to hunt from it on his last morning hunt.

Around 10:30 a.m., the wind was stinging Hartney's face, and he considered leaving his stand and eating lunch. Just then he heard rustling in the woods, and when he looked down, Hartney saw a group of nine does.

The deer milled around, feeding on acorns. Hartney held his breath, hoping a buck would trail the does. One did, but it wasn't what Hartney was looking for. A small 6-pointer arrived and mingled with the does.

Hartney hoped maybe a larger buck would appear and challenge the young buck. Seconds later leaves crunched and twigs snapped, and Hartney's wishful thinking had come true a second time.

A big-bodied buck with a tall, wide rack stepped out from behind a dead tree.

The 6-pointer scampered off, leaving the big boy to watch over the harem of does.

The buck moved closer, effortlessly carrying its rack around low-hanging branches.

When the buck ducked under a pine branch, Hartney raised his shotgun.

The buck moved closer to the does, and when it was 15 yards from Hartney, it stopped. That was all the perched hunter needed, and he placed a slug behind the buck's shoulder. The big 9-pointer dropped.

Kansas Hunter Kills Big Buck

HUNTER: **Tanner Mayhew**
DATE: **2002**
LOCATION: **Kansas**
METHOD: **Bow**
RACK: **10-point buck**

My hunting partner, Aaron, and I headed out for an afternoon bow-hunt in fall 2002.

Aaron decided to hunt the south stand and I went to the one I'd hunted that morning. The ground was soft, and the grass and leaves were limp and quiet. Silently and carefully I worked my way to my stand. Each step was planned and distinct; I wasn't even bothering the birds. As I got closer to the stand, I crouched down low. I figured deer may be sleeping across the creek and they would see me if I stood.

As I got to the stand I tried to keep the tree between me and anything that may be across the creek. Inching up the ladder, I hooked myself to the safety harness. I sat and rested a few minutes before slowly pulling my bow up, being extra careful not to let it hit the ladder or scrape against the tree. I nocked an arrow and laid the bow in my lap and settled in for a long wait.

The sun warmed me in my winter coat, and sleep was pulling at me hard. Then I heard water splashing.

Slowly I turned my head, looking behind me into the creek. Water ripples caught my eyes first, then I saw a deer. I watched it move forward until I couldn't see its head, then I slowly stood and turned around. My beating heart awakened me fully. My eyes widened when I saw the rack. It was a buck — a nice buck!

The sun was somewhat low, reflecting against the water ripples. The wading deer seemed picturesque, like something you would see on a calendar. As it took its time, I carefully and silently attached my pull release to the string hook, all the while wondering if I should take a shot now. The buck strolled down the creek out of range and I hoped it would come back. It disappeared but reappeared on top of the bank 100 yards from me. I knew of a scrape down that way, and that's where I thought it was going.

I prayed to the deer gods in my mind, wishing the buck would come my way. Standing ready, I watched as it moved away from me into the thicket and disappeared from sight. I stayed frozen, studying for any movement. I heard antlers clashing together in the direction of Aaron's stand. Aaron must be rattling, I thought. Maybe that's drawing the buck his way. I saw movement in the bush and tried to focus on it. As I stared, I caught movement back on the trail.

It was the buck! It was circling around and was coming my way.

Quickly I looked back at the brush where I'd seen movement, thinking there's another deer ... maybe bigger. I didn't see anything and turned back to the buck. My eyes danced over it, checking to see if it's worth a shot. Yes, hell yes!

It walked closer and turned to follow the trail that feeds away from me. Its head disappeared behind a tree and I drew my bow. As it walked along, I placed my sight pin right on its shoulder. There, that's it ... no the string ... line up the string. I turned the bow so the string hid the pin sight as I followed the deer. With a touch of my finger the arrow was off. My eyes followed it until it disappeared in the buck.

My eyes were wide, ready to watch which way the buck might dart. To my surprise it didn't jump or run, but trotted down the trail about 50 feet and then stopped. It stood there for a moment, then started to sway. I held my breath. The buck's hind end went down first, and the rest followed.

I kept my eyes on the buck to make sure it didn't get up and run, but I knew it wouldn't.

As I sat waiting, I wondered "what have I done?" I must admit to feeling some guilt for killing this animal. Time crawled, and after 20 minutes I decided that was enough time, and I climbed down.

Finding the buck's trail, I looked up ahead and saw the buck laying there. Slowly I approached, watching for any movement. I know it's dead. Putting my arrow back in the quiver, I looked it over and counted its points. I studied the buck for a while and decided it was time for the four-wheeler, so I went to find Aaron for help. I didn't really want to spoil his hunting, but I figured it would be easier to get the deer out in the daylight.

I walked to the edge of the alfalfa field to whistle at Aaron, and I saw him climb down from his tree stand and start walking. I met him half way. When we got close enough to hear each other I told him "We have meat!"

"What did you get?" he asked.

"It's a buck and he was headed toward your rattling."

"But I didn't bring my antlers to rattle with," he replied.

As we pulled up to the buck, Aaron blurted "That's a nice buck!"

We followed the blood trail back to where I hit the deer, which was easy to do. Aaron paced off the shot at 35 yards.

— Tanner Mayhew

Big Buck Escapes Once, But Hunter Succeeds

HUNTER: **Eric Davidson**
DATE: **Nov. 10, 2002**
LOCATION: **Illinois**
METHOD: **Bow**
RACK: **8-point buck**

Eric Davidson of Joy, Ill., saw a dandy buck twice during Illinois' 2001 bow-season, but both times the buck was out of range. However, Davidson had his heart set on shooting this buck.

The third time Davidson saw the buck, he grunted it into bow-range, and it looked like he was finally going to get a shot at the big farm-country buck.

But there are no guarantees in bow-hunting.

Davidson's grunts drew more than just the big boy. A smaller buck also responded to Davidson's call.

The small buck came in from behind Davidson's stand, and stopped directly below the hunter's tree stand. All Davidson could see of the deer was the young buck's rack below his boots.

Now he was stuck. If he moved, he'd surely spook the little buck, which would also scare the big boy. Although he was heartbroken, Davidson stayed still and watched his quarry disappear. Davidson didn't see the buck the rest of the season.

The 2002 bow-season was a different story. By Nov. 10, the rut was red hot, and Davidson knew it was time to try for the big buck again.

About an hour after daybreak that morning, Davidson spotted a doe, and the big buck was right behind.

Davidson couldn't believe it, but the buck was traveling on the exact trail he predicted it would. Everything was falling perfectly into place.

As the two deer drew closer, the doe saw Davidson, and Davidson thought his hunt was over.

Just then, the buck grunted, and the doe forgot about what it had seen and started walking again.

When the buck passed Davidson's stand, it stopped, giving the hunter the shot he'd been waiting so long for, and Davidson made good on the opportunity.

The big 8-pointer, which was missing both brow tines, dressed out at 245 pounds.

Eleven-Year-Old Kills 17-Point Illinois Buck

It's always a good idea to give young hunters lots of encouragement, but the outlook for Vince Bales' future hunting seasons is pretty bleak. At only 11 years old, he shot a buck the likes of which he may never see again, let alone shoot.

Bales took up deer hunting at age 8. In his first three years of hunting, he killed one deer. But the deer he killed Nov. 22, 2002, is one he just can't stop thinking about.

Bales and his father, Craig, were hunting in Peoria County on opening morning of the Illinois shotgun-season. They had yet to see a deer when at 7:15 a.m., Vince spotted the monster whitetail.

"Dad, there's a deer," he whispered.

The elder hunter slowly swiveled his head and couldn't believe what he saw. The monster whitetail was standing broadside only 12 yards away, looking in away from the two hunters.

HUNTER: **Vince Bales**
DATE: **Nov. 22, 2002**
LOCATION: **Illinois**
METHOD: **Shotgun**
RACK: **17-point buck**

"Wow, I guess that's a deer!" he hissed.

Vince aimed at the buck, but his careful aim was making his father nervous.

"What are you waiting for?" he asked.

The shotgun blast answered his question, and Vince dropped the buck in its tracks with a single shot.

Craig said watching his son shoot the buck was a truly incredible experience.

Vince can't stop talking about the buck, and Craig is very proud of his son's calmness in shooting the impressive whitetail.

The buck sported 17 points and field dressed at 220 pounds. It was 6½ years old.

Luck of the Draw Helps Hunter Tag Booner

Tim Nordengren, of Viroqua, Wis., bagged his 2001 buck partly by the luck of the draw.

Opening day of Wisconsin's 2001 gun-season dawned foggy, severly limiting visibility. Nordengren passed up a forkhorn and some does opening weekend, and had to work during the week. His thoughts drifted to the following weekend.

Nordengren was optimistic about his chances. He hunts an area made up of steep hillsides and thick brush. If the terrain isn't enough to allow bucks to survive, many area landowners practice quality deer management, too. The combination helps bucks grow old and large in Nordengren's area.

HUNTER: **Tim Nordengren**
DATE: **November 2001**
LOCATION: **Wisconsin**
METHOD: **.270 Rifle**
RACK: **13-point buck, 180-class**

The weather the second weekend was no better than the first, and the deer weren't moving.

Nordengren and three other members of his hunting party decided to make the deer move with some drives. The hunters drew cards to decide who would sit and who would drive. Nordengren chose one of the high cards and chose to sit first.

The foursome drove several different areas in Vernon County, but as evening approached, they hadn't bagged a deer.

The group decided to drive some land owned by Nordengren's mother. Over the years several large bucks were shot there.

On the last drive, it was Nordengren's turn to walk. After dropping off the two standers and allowing them about 15 minutes to reach their stands, Nordengren and the other hunter began walking down a hollow. The rain picked up and wind blew in Nordengren's face, making hunting miserable.

Nordengren had just passed one of the standers when a huge buck jumped up 80 yards away. It ran downhill, broadside.

Nordengren shouldered his .270, aimed and fired. The buck acted like it wasn't hit, so Nordengren shot twice more before it vanished over a ravine.

After waiting a few minutes, Nordengren walked to the edge of the ravine. At the bottom was his 13-pointer!

The buck netted 181 4/8 inches.

Maryland Man Fulfills Big-Buck Dream

Ernie Welsh, of Darlington, Md., has dreamed of shooting a record-book buck since he was 10. On Nov. 2, 2002, that dream came true.

Welsh and his hunting partner headed to their stands at 3 p.m. that day for their afternoon bowhunt.

HUNTER: **Ernie Welsh**
DATE: **Nov. 2, 2002**
LOCATION: **Maryland**
METHOD: **Bow**
RACK: **12-point buck, 150-class**

At 4 p.m., several does entered a field near Welsh's deer stand.

Soon, a doe ran out of a thicket 150 yards away, and when Welsh brought his binoculars to his eyes, he saw a huge rack coming toward him through the thick cover.

At first Welsh thought the doe joined the others in the field, but when it realized it was in the thicket, he grew excited. A major trail runs through the thick growth and passes near Welsh's stand.

Both deer disappeared from sight, and for a few anxious minutes, Welsh didn't know what was happening in the thicket, but then the doe appeared about 60 yards away, and Welsh saw those big antlers bobbing in his direction.

Suddenly a fawn ran past Welsh's stand only 10 yards away and stopped. The doe was apparently looking for the fawn and approached Welsh, but from his downwind side. Meanwhile the buck walked into the field about 40 yards away.

Welsh had to make sure he could position himself for a shot as the buck drew closer without alarming the doe.

Welsh looked at the doe to make sure it wasn't watching him, then looked back at the buck, which had its head down. Welsh drew back on the buck. When it was 35 yards out, he launched the arrow. The arrow broke the buck's spine and penetrated the lungs, dropping it instantly.

Welsh radioed his hunting partner, who was equally excited when he saw the wide-racked buck.

Welsh's boyhood dream had finally come true after more than 30 years of hunting. His wide-racked, Pope & Young-class 12-pointer had a 26-inch spread and grossed 158⁵/₈ inches. Welsh's trophy buck field dressed at 191 pounds.

Charles Alsheimer
Western New York, 2002
140-class 10-pointer

Charles J. Alsheimer

Hunter Ends Season But Takes Family Trip

Don Snyder of Sawyer, Mich., faced a dilemma most hunters would envy on Nov. 3, 2002. Snyder had already shot an 8-point buck early in Michigan's archery season. Now, with gun season just days away, he wasn't sure if he should go bow-hunting, because Michigan hunters are only allowed two bucks.

Every year, Snyder's family gets together to hunt in the wilds of Michigan's Upper Peninsula, with family members coming all the way from Washington for the annual hunt. The group lives in a 16-foot-by-32-foot wall tent and enjoys the pleasures of camp life.

HUNTER: **Don Snyder**
DATE: **Nov. 3, 2002**
LOCATION: **Michigan**
METHOD: **Bow**
RACK: **8-point buck**

However, on Nov. 3, Snyder decided to head for his stand in the corner of two fence lines, and surrounded by woods and cornfields. Nothing said he had to use his second buck tag. But one thing was for certain. Any buck he saw would have to be bigger than the first buck he'd shot that season, otherwise he'd wait for gun season.

At first light Snyder rattled aggressively, but got no response. At about 8:45, Snyder saw a doe, and was satisfied with his morning hunt after seeing a deer. But things were going to get even better.

At about 9:10, two deer walked through the fence row to the edge of the corn. The first was a good buck, but the other deer kept its head down. Both deer disappeared into the corn.

Snyder reached for his rattling antlers and tickled them together, startled by the loud noise they made on a crisp, clear morning.

Within a minute a nice 8-pointer materialized and walked directly toward Snyder. It was looking side to side, trying to find the fighting deer.

The buck went behind a tree, giving Snyder a chance to draw. When the buck was 12 yards away, Snyder grunted and the buck stopped. Snyder launched the arrow, which found its mark behind the buck's shoulder. The buck crashed through the corn and fell 40 yards away.

Snyder was pleased with the 160-pound 8-pointer, and hunted with his video camera on his trip to the Upper Peninsula.

Pistol Hunter Downs State Record Nontypical

Sometimes when opportunity knocks, the door slams behind you. At least that's what happened to Michael Culley and his family and friends.

Culley's party hunts on a 1,200-acre farm in Indiana. They had hunted there for years, and one year asked the neighbors if they could park their vehicles on the adjoining property. Not only did the neighbors allow them to park, they allowed them to hunt the property, too.

HUNTER: **Michael Culley**
DATE: **November 2001**
LOCATION: **Indiana**
METHOD: **.45-70 Gov. Pistol**
RACK: **23-point buck, 220-class**

Culley's father spotted a big buck while bow-hunting the week before gun season, so the hunting party was optimistic.

Deer hunting is a family event for Culley, and many relatives get together over Thanksgiving for the hunt. In fact, each year, 12 to 15 hunters chip in $20 apiece for the family big buck contest. The winner takes home the pot and a traveling plaque.

Culley's uncle had came from Tennessee for Thanksgiving. Culley tried to persuade him to stay for an extra day or two, but he couldn't. Culley decided to hunt out of his uncle's permanent tree stand the following morning.

About 10 a.m., Culley saw a giant buck about 80 yards away. He drew his T/C .45-70 Gov. and fired. The buck ran down a ravine and crashed after running about 50 yards. However, it was still alive and Culley shot again to kill it.

After Culley's announcement on the radio, everyone rushed over to see Culley's buck.

Culley was calm when making his way to his buck, but when he arrived, he was speechless, as was the rest of his group.

The monster nontypical sported 23 points, including a 12$^{1}/_{2}$-inch drop tine. It scores 223$^{2}/_{8}$ Boone and Crockett inches, and ranks as Indiana's new pistol record nontypical.

Culley's uncle has informed everyone he *will* be staying for the day after Thanksgiving this year, and the group joked that Culley can't hunt next year after bagging the monster.

However, they weren't far from wrong. After news of the giant spread, the neighbors decided not to allow Culley's group to hunt on their property this year. Culley's group still plans to hunt the other farm.

Man Finds Silver Lining In Botched Opportunity

Many hunters have experienced that sickening feeling of missing a wall-hanger buck. Jim Luppens of Suffolk, N.Y. must have felt it Nov. 7, 2002.

On that day, he had a shot at an 8-pointer, but shot over the buck's back.

The next day, Luppens hunted from a new stand. He practiced the same routine he'd repeated so many mornings already that archery season: get up at 4 a.m., load up the hunting gear, head off into the darkness and hope that today is the day.

Well, that *was* the day.

HUNTER: **Jim Luppens**
DATE: **Nov. 8, 2002**
LOCATION: **New York**
METHOD: **Bow**
RACK: **10-point buck, 170-class**

Luppens climbed into his stand in a small, briar-choked woodlot, being careful to make as little noise as possible.

Shortly after settling into his climber, Luppens heard deer moving through the woods around him.

At 6:45 a.m., he spotted a doe heading his way. When the doe got closer, Luppens saw the deer's sides heaving and its tongue lolling. It was obvious to Luppens that the doe was being chased by a buck.

As soon as the doe disappeared, Luppens heard a deep, guttural tending grunt.

The buck was about 70 yards away when Luppens first saw it, and it looked like it would pass by Luppens' stand out of bow-range. That's when Luppens remembered the grunt call hanging around his neck.

Luppens blew a couple deep grunts and the rutting buck stopped in its tracks, looking for the intruder.

The buck trotted right toward Luppens. When it was about 22 yards away, Luppens finally got a good look at the buck's tall, wide rack.

Luppens didn't stare at the buck's antlers long, and instead, concentrated on a single tuft of hair behind the big 10-pointer's shoulder.

Luppens' shot went through the buck's lungs and angled through its liver.

A 100-yard tracking job led Luppens to his whopper 10-pointer, which had a 21 1/8-inch spread and grossed 170 7/8 inches. The buck also sported a pair of foot-high tines and field dressed at 192 pounds.

Hunter Tags Best Buck Before Grandpa's death

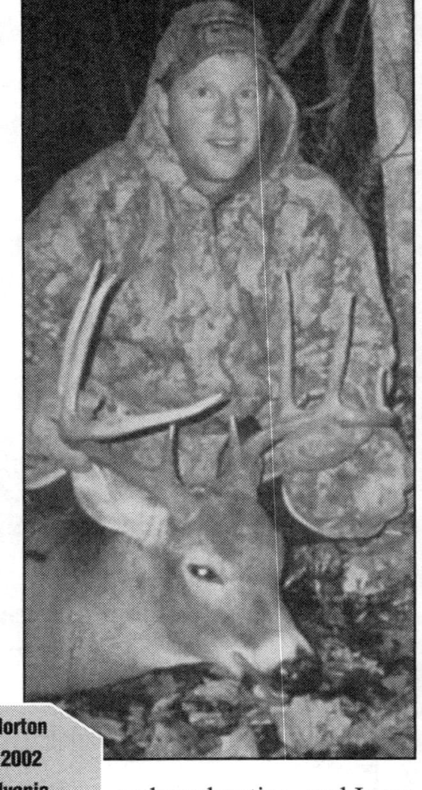

HUNTER:	**Kerry Morton**
DATE:	**Nov. 2, 2002**
LOCATION:	**Pennsylvania**
METHOD:	**Bow**
RACK:	**10-point buck**

Nov. 2, 2002, dawned cold and snowy. It was the kind of morning that you anticipate throughout archery season. During the summer months my hunting partner, Kevin Brubaker, and I had seen some nice bucks, so we were optimistic about the upcoming season. We planned to hunt a place where Kevin had seen a nice buck the night before.

The weather that morning made it difficult to stay in the stand very long. We both saw the buck, but neither of us got a shot. At around 9:30 a.m. we decided to go back to the cabin to warm up a bit, then head back out.

It is difficult to leave your stand on a promising morning, but the cold weather took its toll. At around 10:30 I went to a different location to hunt. I climbed into my tree about 11 a.m. About a half-hour later I saw a deer approach, but it was just a yearling.

Because it was also small game season, I knew there would be activity in the woods, so I knew I had to stay on stand as long as possible to take advantage of deer that might be pushed by small game hunters.

Through time spent fishing and hunting with my grandfather, I learned that patience has its rewards. And that statement is never truer than when it comes to archery hunting, and I was going to be reminded about that again today.

Around 1 p.m. I was contemplating going back to the cabin to get warm and have something to eat. I had not seen any deer for about two hours. Due to the weather conditions it was a hard decision to make, but I decided to stay in the stand.

Around 1:30 I spotted some deer coming toward my stand. It turned out to be two does and two fawns.

Over the years my grandfather told me there is a good chance a buck could be chasing does, so when I see a doe, I remain patient.

Soon after that I saw some deer running on a hillside behind me. That was now six does — I had to see a buck sooner or later.

About 15 minutes later I saw another deer coming toward my stand. I could not see it clearly, so I assumed it was another doe.

The deer stepped out from behind a big oak tree, and much to my surprise, my heart just about stopped beating. I can usually control myself, but when I saw the size of this buck, it was hard to keep my composure. My grandfather has harvested some nice bucks in his lifetime, so when I saw this buck I could appreciate the excitement that he had experienced.

When I first saw the buck, it was about 90 yards away. If you have done much archery hunting, you will understand when I say that is when the hunt begins.

The buck was very cautious, but I had done some scouting before season and figured my stand location was good.

When the buck started to approach my stand it would stop about every five yards to test the wind. Every time it stopped, I thought my heart was going to explode.

It took about 5 minutes for the buck to come into bow-range. At about 25 yards it stopped and faced directly toward me. I knew it had to turn to give me a better-shot.

Finally it turned broadside when it was about 20 to 25 yards away, and I released the arrow. I figured I'd made a good hit, so I called Kevin on the radio and told him I'd just shot a monster buck. He asked me if I had retrieved the arrow to see if it was a good hit.

"I am shaking too badly to climb out of my tree stand," I replied.

Anybody who has killed a trophy whitetail knows the feelings I was having at the time. I decided to go back to the cabin and discuss the situation with Kevin.

We decided to give the buck time to bed down. This is one more lesson that my grandfather taught me. Through the years we have had our differences of opinion when it came to bow-hunting, but I still feel he gave me some very useful tips. I will dearly miss sharing my hunting stories with him.

When we recovered my 10-pointer, to say I was on top of the world is an understatement. Kevin and my wife can testify to that. My first thought was to get to my grandfather's house to share my story with him.

My grandfather was very interested in hearing my story and congratulated me on my success. I know he was proud of my accomplishment because he told a lot of people about it. Sadly, he passed away 11 days later at the age of 90.

Due to the fact that I got to share the story of my best buck with my grandfather just before his death, this is my most memorable buck.

— Kerry Morton

Third Time's a Charm On Big 14-Pointer

HUNTER:	**Levone Boggs**
DATE:	**Nov. 14, 2002**
LOCATION:	**South Carolina**
METHOD:	**7 mm Rifle**
RACK:	**14-point buck**

The 2002 hunting season was a memorable one for Levone Boggs of Belton, S.C. Early in the season he shot an 8-pointer that weighed more than 200 pounds.

Little did he know his season was about to get even better.

On Nov. 7, Boggs was hunting from his tree stand on about 70 acres of forested land. His stand was situated in the woods, overlooking a pipeline right of way.

A doe appeared about 250 yards away, and right behind it was a huge buck. Boggs raised his 7 mm, found the buck in his scope, and pulled the trigger. The buck mule-kicked, ran 5 yards and stopped. Boggs shot again and the deer ran.

Boggs didn't know what to think. He assumed he must have hit the buck on the first shot, judging by the buck's reaction, but he couldn't explain why it stopped.

When Boggs reached the place where the buck had been standing, he found hair, but no blood. Despite his best efforts, Boggs couldn't find any sign of where the buck had traveled, and he left the woods disappointed.

The following evening, he brought along Troy Moss, a 13-year-old boy from the neighborhood. Boggs and his family enjoy taking kids hunting. Boggs and Moss climbed into tree stands a few feet apart.

Once again a doe appeared, and limping behind her was the same buck Boggs had shot at the day before! Moss didn't see the deer, so Boggs whistled to alert him. Though his plan worked, the noise also alerted the doe. The doe stopped and saw Moss as he positioned himself for a shot, and the two deer ran off.

On Nov. 14, Boggs was once again sitting in his stand. His morning hunt was a good one. First he saw a 6-pointer, then a spike. After the spike disappeared from view, Boggs got comfortable in his stand and took a 15-minute nap. When he awoke, the big buck was staring at him!

Or so he thought. Boggs later learned the buck was staring at a doe under his tree, but it didn't matter. The buck was there, and Boggs shot. The deer took five steps and fell.

Boggs' 14-pointer had a live weight of 185 pounds and green-scored 152$^{7}/_{8}$ inches. Boggs' shot on Nov. 7 had hit the 14-pointer in the front leg.

Drop-Tine Dream Buck Sparks Many Emotions

HUNTER: **Robert Boroski**
DATE: **Nov. 22, 2002**
LOCATION: **West Virginia**
METHOD: **Bow**
RACK: **9-point buck**

Robert Boroski of Princeton, W.Va., will never forget the highs and lows he experienced on Nov. 14, 2002.

Boroski was bow-hunting public land in southern West Virginia with his son, Todd, and friend, Kevin Graham. Rutting activity was up, and cold weather was finally arriving.

Boroski was hunting a funnel at the bottom of three ridges, and his partners were hunting near each other about 3/4 mile away.

Boroski didn't see any deer early that morning, but radio checks with his companions were promising. Todd and Kevin had seen bucks, and Kevin missed one. Boroski was optimistic about his chances of seeing deer, especially because most deer sightings from his funnel stand are after 9 a.m.

Five minutes after getting off the radio at 9 a.m., Boroski saw movement. A big buck was making its way to Boroski's stand. However, it stopped to feed on acorns for what seemed like forever. Finally, it neared, and Boroski coaxed it in with his grunt call.

However, the antlers had Boroski "all shook up," and though he reminded his partners to ignore antlers when shooting, he couldn't heed his own advice after seeing his dream buck's 9-inch drop tine.

Boroski struggled to draw his bow on the buck. When he shot, he watched his arrow sail harmlessly over the buck's back, and his dream buck disappear.

His partners could tell how depressed Boroski was about missing the deer, and didn't give him any grief.

On Nov. 22, Boroski returned to the same stand at about 9 a.m. and vowed to hunt all day.

At about noon, two does appeared, followed 15 minutes later by another doe and a 3-pointer.

Minutes later the drop-tine buck appeared. Boroski stayed calm this time and drew the buck in with grunts and doe bleats.

The buck was about 38 yards away, but this time Boroski's shot was right on, and Boroski's dream buck only went 15 yards before falling.

KIM GIBBS of Custer, Wis., saw this buck from her driveway. She slipped out of her house and shot it!

7

Strange Places

Rural Hunter Shoots Back-Yard Bruiser

Kim Gibbs of Custer, Wis., has hunted for the past 10 years, but in the last five years it has been difficult for her and her husband to hunt because they have two young children.

By the fifth day of Wisconsin's 2002 nine-day gun season, Gibbs' tag was yet unfilled, and things weren't looking promising. She had to work until 2 p.m. and was supposed to pick up her children from their baby sitter at 3 p.m.

She rushed to pick up her kids, then went to the bank and the grocery store. Frazzled, she wished that she'd just see a buck in the field as she drove down her long driveway so she could end her season.

Amazingly, that's exactly what happened! A buck and a few does were feeding in the clover field Gibbs' husband had planted!

Gibbs hoped the buck wouldn't spook as she drove to the garage. The children were behaving well, so Gibbs gathered her gear and her rifle and slipped out the back door. To her relief, the buck was still grazing on the clover and showed no sign that it had been disturbed by her presence.

Gibbs waited for the buck to take a few steps so she would have a good shot, and when its vitals were exposed, she pulled the trigger. The buck ran and Gibbs shot again, and when the buck turned toward the woods, Gibbs heard it fall.

Gibbs cautiously walked to where the buck had been, and quickly found her beautiful 8-point buck with a 16-inch inside spread.

Gibbs' brother was just coming out of his stand from back in the woods, and Gibbs gave him a big high five and let out a war whoop.

"So this is what it feels like when you guys get the big one!" she exclaimed.

When her husband came home from hunting two miles down the road, he was stunned to hear that his wife had bagged a respectable buck literally in their back yard.

After examining the rack, they determined that Gibbs' buck was the same deer they'd videotaped just two days before season opened.

New Bow, Mentality Rekindle Passion

Paul Humbert of Brookhaven, N.Y., had become a disgruntled bow-hunter. Housing developments and increasing numbers of nuisance deer permits had pretty much ruined bow-hunting for Humbert on Long Island. But after almost 10 years without bow-hunting, Humbert bought a bow and hoped to rekindle the thrill of bow-hunting.

HUNTER: **Paul Humbert**
DATE: **October 2001**
LOCATION: **New York**
METHOD: **Bow**
RACK: **14-point buck**

Humbert adapted to development, seeking small woodlots and overlooked fringe areas. He found four such areas and hung stands in three of them before season. The fourth area didn't seem too promising, but he gave it a look. Sign was everywhere!

Humbert quickly hung a stand and left the area. The Long Island bow season opened earlier than usual in 2001, and Humbert hoped to cash in on some evening hunts before daylight savings time ended. Unfortunately, he was required to work overtime in October, and didn't get out much.

However, one Sunday evening, Humbert hunted his promising stand. Less than an hour into the hunt Humbert saw a buck heading his way. Humbert hadn't expected to see a deer from the buck's direction and hadn't cut any shooting lanes. What's more, the deer was quartering downwind.

Humbert drew his bow, arched around the tree and picked an opening. When the buck finally picked his way into the lane 25 yards away, Humbert released.

Humbert thought it was a good hit, but the deer ran toward a nearby road with houses on the other side. He hoped the deer wouldn't cross.

When Humbert examined his shaft, he was disappointed. It appeared to be a gut shot. Humbert left the deer overnight.

The next morning he was eager to recover his buck. He found a good blood trail for 75 yards, but it stopped. He decided to call Deer Search, and an hour later Lee Behrens arrived with her beagle. The dog also lost the trail.

Still, Humbert wouldn't give up. Gerard German and his friend Nino joined the search that afternoon. They parked at the opposite side of the woods a half-mile from Humbert's stand and zig-zagged across the property. Light was fading when Nino yelled, "Come get your buck!"

Humbert thought he was joking, but 60 yards away under a bush was Humbert's buck!

Daniel Schmidt
Central Wisconsin, Oct. 12, 2002
130-class 9-pointer

Daniel E. Schmidt

Rhode Island Hunt Unfolds in 'Small World'

For Jason Richer of North Smithfield, R.I., the 2000 muzzleloader season was a dramatic series of luck and coincidences.

Richer's wife was expecting their third child right around the opening of Rhode Island's muzzleloader season, despite the fact Richer had received a vasectomy. This put a serious damper on Richer's hunting. He hunts 45 miles from home, and what Rhode Island lacks in acreage, it makes up for in traffic, Richer said. On a bad traffic day, that drive could take 2 hours.

HUNTER: **Jason Richer**
DATE: **2000**
LOCATION: **Rhode Island**
METHOD: **Muzzleloader**
RACK: **9-point buck**

Finally, a week before the season opened, Richer's wife convinced him to hunt near home and carry a radio. Begrudgingly, Richer decided any hunting was better than sitting home wishing he was hunting.

Richer located a 300-acre woodlot in a suburban area and secured permission to hunt it. On his scouting trip days before the season, he found little sign, and his hunting partner, Steve Voisinet, opted to hunt their traditional hunting grounds, saying "Your wife is pregnant, not mine." However, Voisinet said Richer could call him if he needed help dragging a deer out.

Opening day began with a lackluster start. It took Richer an hour to find a suitable tree for his climbing tree stand, and he didn't get set up until an hour after daylight. Plus, he felt uneasy hunting 600 feet from houses, many of which were homes to anti-hunters.

Things brightened a bit when a doe appeared a half-hour after Richer set up. Richer passed, but after a couple hours without seeing another deer, he began second-guessing himself. However, his patience was rewarded when the woods grew loud with the sound of approaching deer, and soon a herd of seven does and five bucks emerged from a ravine 100 yards away.

The largest buck was busy corralling the does and chasing away the other bucks. Three times the big buck chased the does, then stopped behind the same tree, preventing Richer from getting a shot. Finally, the buck stopped in the open 125 yards away and Richer fired. The buck was knocked off balance, recovered, and ran downhill.

After the deer disappeared, Richer scanned the area, and to his horror, realized a branch had broken off in his line of fire. Now he didn't know what to think, although the buck acted hit.

After waiting a half-hour, an 8-pointer that had been part of the herd appeared, chasing does. Maybe the big buck was down, Richer hoped. However, he waited another half-hour before climbing down from his tree to investigate.

Richer climbed down and began his search, but found no blood or hair, and following the buck's tracks amidst all the others was impossible. He decided to call for help.

On his hike back to his truck, he saw a long-lost cousin raking leaves in the suburban area. He told Richer it was OK to cut across his property, which shaved a quarter-mile off Richer's hike.

An hour later, Richer, his wife, Voisinet, and his wife returned to search for the buck.

Voisinet located the buck's bed and found a bit of blood, then four drops after the buck exited its bed.

The crew scoured the area for more sign, and finally, Voisinet found another spot of blood 300 yards from the bed. Suddenly, the buck sprang from its bed 20 yards away. It fell twice, then Voisinet shot it. It fell again, then ran off as if it wasn't injured. However, the buck was now leaving a heavy blood trail, but now it was headed for private property.

State law prohibits carrying weapons onto property on which you do not have permission to hunt on, but you can trail a wounded deer unarmed. Richer and Voisinet left their weapons with their wives and continued trailing the buck. The trail led across a newly paved driveway and finally into the backyard of an upscale home.

The trackers decided to ask permission of the homeowner to track the buck, which they thought was down near his tennis court. Although he wasn't happy about it, he was impressed they had so diligently stuck with the blood trail, and granted Richer and Voisinet permission. Their wives showed up just in time because the buck was not dead and required a finishing shot.

Richer felt sick, surrounded by anti-hunters and thought about giving up hunting at that moment. The landowner and his wife watched the spectacle, and Richer felt pretty low about how things turned out. Things became a little brighter when Voisinet realized the landowner's wife was his dentist.

As Richer and Voisinet loaded the buck into Richer's truck, a car pulled in — it was Richer's cousin again, who had a dinner date with the landowner and his wife!

The landowner and his wife were impressed with Richer's persistence, and gave him access to their property on future hunts.

Richer's 9-pointer had a $21^{2}/_{8}$-inch inside spread and dressed at 198 pounds. Richer's son was born 8 days later.

Kyle Franson
Anticosti Island, Quebec
6-pointer

Kyle Franson

Indiana Hunter Finds Big Buck in Small Place

HUNTER: **Kevin Bumbalough**
DATE: **Nov. 16, 1999**
LOCATION: **Indiana**
METHOD: **Shotgun**
RACK: **11-point buck**

In Fall 1999, Kevin Bumbalough had a staircase installed in his Connersville, Ind., home.

Bumbalough and the contractor became good friends, and eventually the contractor asked him if he wanted to hunt on his farm.

Bumbalough asked him how big his farm was, and the contractor told him 10 acres.

Bumbalough was hesitant at first. He didn't think he had much chance of filling his tag on such small acreage, but he decided to give the place a look anyway.

The day before deer season, he checked out the place. It was largely pasture land, but it contained a few tree-lined ditches. The ditches led to a larger woodlot on the adjoining property.

Bumbalough found a fence crossing and began following the deer trail when he discovered a large rub on a cedar tree. Farther down the trail he discovered a twin to the first rub, and 100 yards farther he found a third rub. He speculated the buck that made the rubs scent-checked does in the pasture after dark because the contractor said he saw does in the area, but no bucks. Bumbalough guessed the buck bedded in the woods on the neighbor's property. He reasoned his best chance was to intercept the buck early in the morning on its way from the pasture to the bedding area.

The first few days the wind was wrong for Bumbalough to hunt the area, but on the fourth day he got the north wind he was looking for. Bumbalough was in his tree stand an hour before daylight. The sky was just turning pink when something told Bumbalough to look behind him. When he turned he saw a deer moving through the trees. Upon further inspection he saw big antlers.

Bumbalough doe bleated with his mouth and the buck stopped. Bumbalough touched the trigger on his shotgun. The buck bounded off on a death run and piled up after traveling 30 yards.

Bumbalough began to shake after he saw the big buck fall. After he collected himself, he climbed down and admired his 11-point buck a while before field-dressing it.

Then he called the contractor on his cell phone to show him his big buck shot on small acreage!

12-Pointer Falls On Gas Line Right of Way

Mike Burbey of Sherman, N.Y., was returning from a waterfowl hunt in October 2002 when he spotted a buck feeding with nine does behind a friend's house. At the time he wasn't sure how big the buck was, but he decided to set up in the area and hunt the deer.

A few days later, Burbey returned to the area to scout and hang a stand. He placed his stand on a ridge overlooking a rub line above a thick creek bottom.

HUNTER: **Mike Burbey**
DATE: **Nov. 6, 2002**
LOCATION: **New York**
METHOD: **Bow**
RACK: **12-point buck**

Things started slowly at Burbey's new stand. After his first two evening hunts, he'd only seen one doe. However, Burbey knew the buck was in the area because several more large rubs had appeared within 20 yards of his stand.

On Nov. 6, the wind was right for Burbey to hunt the stand again. It was overcast and the temperature was in the low 30s and falling.

Burbey had sat for three hours with no deer sightings. After finishing a rattling and grunting sequence, he spotted a buck traveling on a gas line right of way about 80 yards away. Burbey had used this right of way to enter his stand and had walked in using a scent drag. When the buck hit the scent trail, it turned and began following it toward Burbey's stand.

Burbey still didn't realize how big the buck was. He just noticed it had branched antlers, and he prepared to shoot.

When the buck was 25 yards away, it turned onto a trail that would bring it within 10 yards of Burbey's stand. The buck was upwind and everything looked promising.

When the buck passed behind a small bush, Burbey drew, and when it stepped into the open, he launched his arrow and made a good hit. Only when the buck trotted off did Burbey realize how big it was.

After carefully getting out of his stand in his excitement, Burbey followed the blood trail for 60 yards to his 12-pointer. The deer died on the gas line right of way and required no dragging!

Hunter Takes First Buck In His Own Back Yard

James Lakoduk of Warroad, Minn., hunted for seven seasons without shooting a buck. He'd seen small bucks, but he wanted his first buck to be a big one.

He couldn't hunt opening weekend of muzzleloader season, but he planned to hunt Tuesday morning. After getting off of work at 6 a.m., he headed for his stand for a morning hunt.

When he got to the stand, he realized he didn't have his keys to get in. He returned home to get his brother's keys, but he was sleeping, so he returned to the stand and sat on the ground.

HUNTER: **James Lakoduk**
DATE: **Dec. 3, 2002**
LOCATION: **Minnesota**
METHOD: **Muzzleloader**
RACK: **10-point buck**

Lakoduk saw five does and two small bucks, but by 11:00, the 8-degree weather got to him, so he went home to warm up.

Lakoduk lives on the edge of the Beltrami State Forest and deer frequently walk through his yard. Lakoduk made himself some lunch and watched for deer out the window.

Soon he saw a nice buck, so he grabbed his muzzleloader and ran outside. The buck was only 60 yards away, but Lakoduk saw it was a 7-pointer. His family passes on bucks smaller than 8 points, so he let the buck walk.

Lakoduk stared out the window all day. When his brother finally awoke, there wasn't enough time to make it to the stand before dark, but the deer were moving. Lakoduk remained at the window.

At 4:20 three does walked across the driveway, checking their back trail. Finally the same 7-pointer emerged from the woods, and soon after, another, bigger buck entered the yard.

Lakoduk grabbed his muzzleloader, put a musket cap on and raced outside. The buck was 70 yards away when Lakoduk shouldered the gun, composed himself and started to count points. When he got to 8 he stopped counting and pulled the trigger. Lakoduk went back inside and got his jacket, gloves and knife and returned to trail the buck.

Lakoduk's first buck, a 10-pointer, had gone 50 yards before dropping.

Leonard Lee Rue III

8

Big Buck References

Insights May Help Tag Your Dream Buck

We deer hunters, in our continuing efforts to learn more about white-tailed deer and deer hunting, are constant seekers of information.

We spend late nights poring over our hunting camp journals, digest every issue of our favorite deer hunting magazines and watch all the latest hunting videos.

And that's just when we're not hunting or scouting!

This chapter is packed with insights to help you kill your dream buck, wherever your quest may lead you.

Also included are handy references to help you process your buck's statistics once you've gotten it, such as *Deer & Deer Hunting's* white-tailed deer aging poster and a sample Boone & Crockett scoring sheet.

Also included are details about our most respected big-game record-keeping organizations, the Boone & Crockett Club and the Pope & Young Club, and their contact information.

You'll also find a map produced by the Quality Deer Management Association that breaks down all B&C and P&Y entries from 1991 to 2000 by county, giving you a quick reference as to which counties produce the most record-class bucks.

In recent years much research has been done in determining how the moon affects rutting behavior. You'll find 2003-2004 full-moon dates, as well as background on the moon's effects on deer. If that whets your appetite for more, you'll learn about valuable sources of more information on how the moon affects rutting behavior.

If your next hunting adventure takes you far from home, we've included state wildlife agency contact information, as well as tips for the traveling deer hunter. Also included are things you need to know before planning your trip to the Canadian bush, and details of dealing with heightened airport security after 9/11.

Rounding out the chapter, Daniel E. Schmidt's article, "Myles Keller's Whitetail Tactics: Why Scouting is More Critical than Hunting," reveals scouting tips from a legendary bow-hunter.

How to Age a White-tailed Deer

Biologists and deer researchers agree that analysis of tooth replacement and wear — though not perfect — is the most handy and reliable field method for aging whitetails. That's because, regardless of where they live, whitetails lose their baby "milk" teeth and wear out their permanent teeth on a fairly predictable schedule.

At birth, white-tailed fawns have four teeth. Adult deer have 32 teeth — 12 premolars, 12 molars, six incisors and two canines.

Aging analysis often is based on the wear of the molars, which lose about 1 millimeter of height per year. It takes a deer about 10½ years to wear its teeth down to the gum line. Therefore, it's difficult to determine the age of a deer that's older than 10½ years.

Most importantly, the ability to estimate a deer's age based on the wear of its teeth is something most hunters can learn with a little study and practice.

To order a full-color poster of our complete guide to tooth aging, call (888) 457-2873.

Instructions: Cut one side of the deer's jaw all the way to its socket. Prop open the jaws and compare the lower jaw to these photos to estimate the deer's age.

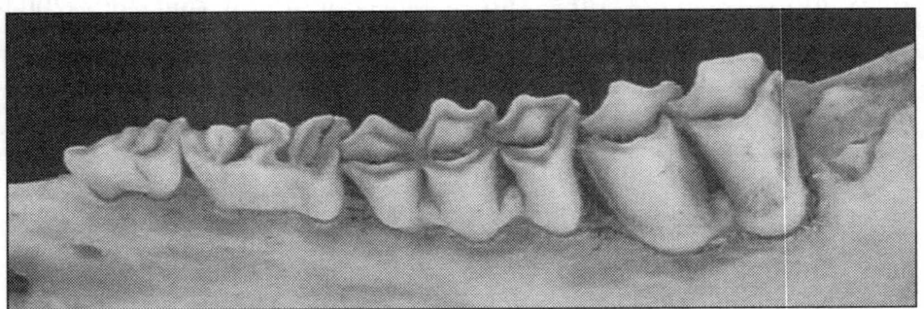

Fawn

Few hunters have difficulty aging a white-tailed fawn, whose short snout and small body are usually obvious when viewed up close. If there is doubt, simply count the teeth in the deer's lower jaw. If the jaw has less than six teeth, the deer is a fawn.

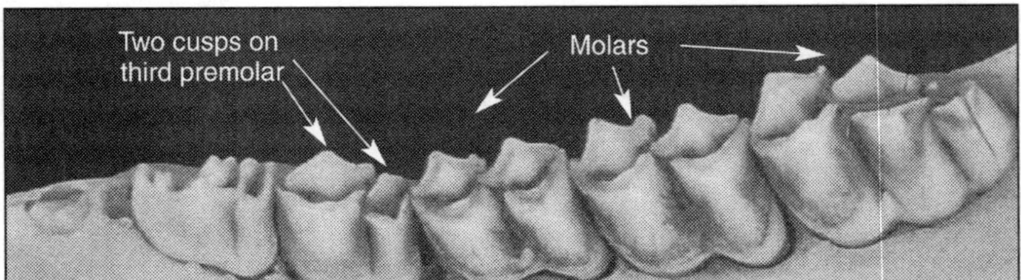

Yearling: At Least 19 Months

About 1 year, 7 months, most deer have all three permanent premolars. The new teeth are white in contrast to pigmentation on older teeth. They have a smooth, chalk-white appearance and show no wear. The third molar is partially erupted.

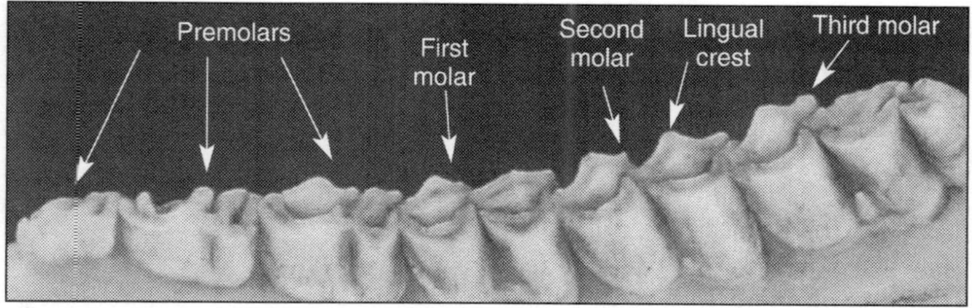

2½ Years

The lingual crests of the first molar are sharp, with the enamel rising well above the narrow dentine (the dark layer below the enamel) of the crest. Crests on the first molar are as sharp as those on the second and third molar. Wear on the posterior cusp of the third molar is slight, and the gum line is often not retracted enough to expose the full height of this cusp.

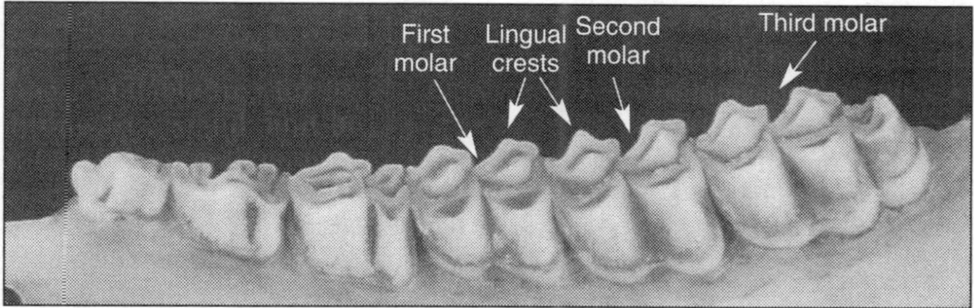

3½ Years

The lingual crests (inside, next to tongue) of the first molar are blunted, and the dentine of the crests on this tooth is as wide or wider than the enamel. Compare it to the second molar. The dentine on the second molar is not wider than the enamel, which means this deer is probably 3½ years old. Also, the posterior cusp of the third molar is flattened by wear, forming a definite concavity on the biting surface of the teeth.

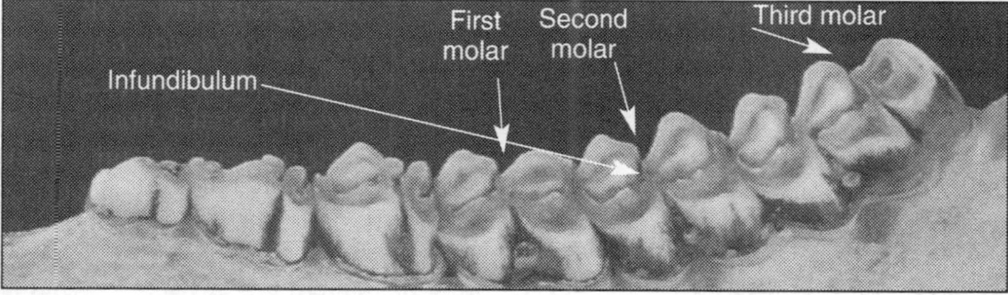

4½ to 5½ Years

At this point, it's often hard to distinguish between the two age classes. The lingual crests of the first molar are almost worn away. The posterior cusp of the third molar is worn at the cusp's edge so the biting surface slopes downward. Wear has spread to the second molar, making the dentine wider than the enamel on first and second molars. By age 5½ wear has usually spread to all six teeth, making the dentine wider than the enamel on all teeth. Because the first molar is the oldest, it wears out first. Also, by 5½, there might be no lingual crests on the first and second molars, although rounded edges might appear like crests. A line drawn from lingual to outside edges of first and second molars generally touches the enamel on both sides of the infundibulum.

Bow-Hunting Receives Boost from Pope and Young Club

The formation of the Pope and Young Club arose from a need to show the world the bow was an effective, viable hunting tool. Most hunters and state game agencies of the 1940s and 1950s believed the bow was little more than a toy, and few recognized it as a hunting weapon.

It was Glenn St. Charles and a group of dedicated bow-hunters who conceived the idea of pulling together all the nationwide bow-hunting successes they could document. Their idea was to bring all of the information together and show it to those who believed bow-hunting was ineffective.

Today, the bow is accepted nationwide.

Although few people in the non-hunting world think of the hunter as a conservationist, the hunter has always been one. Aldo Leopold, the father of the modern conservation ethic, was a bow-hunter and advocate of land stewardship. It was Theodore Roosevelt — an avid hunter — who conceived the idea of the Boone and Crockett Club, of which P&Y is modeled after.

— Reprinted courtesy of the Pope and Young Club

Will Your Big Buck Make The Books?

The Boone and Crockett scoring system, with few changes, is essentially the same one developed by a committee of Boone and Crockett Club members and staff in 1950. The system was developed in the 1940s with valuable additions by Grancel Fitz. It was Fitz, who had his own scoring system, that emphasized antler symmetry in the rack's final score.

A B&C score chart for typical-antlered bucks is included on the facing page.

For B&C record-keeping purposes, official scores can be disputed, even years after the original measurement. Repeat measurements are allowed because of the enduring nature of white-tailed deer antlers.

Scoring a rack begins with careful reading of the official score charts reproduced in this book. Be sure to follow the instructions carefully. After taking a rough measurement, the owner must contact a volunteer B&C measurer to get an official measurement for the records program.

An official measurement cannot be made until the rack has dried 60 days after the date of kill. A drying period is necessary to allow for normal shrinkage. The drying period also ensures shrinkage will be relatively the same for all trophies, an impossible condition if "green" scores were allowed.

Where to Write

For more information on white-tailed deer records, contact:

Boone and Crockett Club
The Old Milwaukee Depot
250 Station Drive
Missoula, MT 59801
Phone: (406) 542-1888

Pope and Young Club
15 E. Second St., Box 548
Chatfield, MN 55923
Phone: (507) 867-4144

Boone and Crockett Score Sheet

OFFICIAL SCORING SYSTEM FOR NORTH AMERICAN BIG GAME TROPHIES

Records of North American Big Game

BOONE AND CROCKETT CLUB®

250 Station Drive
Missoula, MT 59801
(406) 542-1888

Minimum Score:	Awards	All-time
whitetail	160	170
Coues'	100	110

TYPICAL
WHITETAIL AND COUES' DEER

Kind of Deer: ______

G2 G3 G4 G5 G6 G7
H4 H3 F E H2 E G1 H1
C B E E D E
Detail of Point Measurement

Abnormal Points	
Right Antler	Left Antler
Subtotals	
Total to E	

SEE OTHER SIDE FOR INSTRUCTIONS				Column 1	Column 2	Column 3	Column 4
A. No. Points on Right Antler		No. Points on Left Antler		Spread Credit	Right Antler	Left Antler	Difference
B. Tip to Tip Spread		C. Greatest Spread					
D. Inside Spread of Main Beams		(Credit May Equal But Not Exceed Longer Antler)					
E. Total of Lengths of Abnormal Points							
F. Length of Main Beam							
G-1. Length of First Point							
G-2. Length of Second Point							
G-3. Length of Third Point							
G-4. Length of Fourth Point, If Present							
G-5. Length of Fifth Point, If Present							
G-6. Length of Sixth Point, If Present							
G-7. Length of Seventh Point, If Present							
H-1. Circumference at Smallest Place Between Burr and First Point							
H-2. Circumference at Smallest Place Between First and Second Points							
H-3. Circumference at Smallest Place Between Second and Third Points							
H-4. Circumference at Smallest Place Between Third and Fourth Points							
TOTALS							

ADD	Column 1		Exact Locality Where Killed:
	Column 2		Date Killed: Hunter:
	Column 3		Owner: Telephone #:
	Subtotal		Owner's Address:
SUBTRACT Column 4			Guide's Name and Address:
FINAL SCORE			Remarks: (Mention Any Abnormalities or Unique Qualities)

(Sample — Not for Official Use)

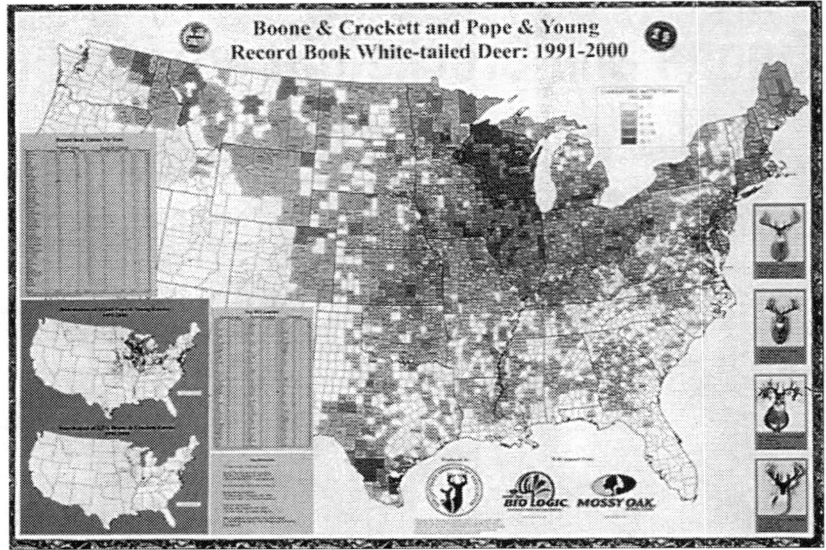

Quality Deer Management Association Offers Map of Record-Class Whitetail Kill Densities

Have you ever wondered which areas produce the most Boone and Crockett and Pope and Young bucks? Well, today, answering that question is easier than ever, thanks to detailed maps compiled by the Quality Deer Management Association.

The maps, created by QDMA intern Joel Helmer, reflect how many record-class bucks each county in the Unites States produced from 1991 to 2000. To illustrate concentrations of record-class buck kills registered with B&C and P&Y during the 10-year period, each county is color-coded in shades of red, with the darkest shade indicating the most big-buck kills.

The map reveals some fascinating aspects of how geography, climate and soil conditions affect deer size. For example, some of the highest concentrations of record-class bucks have been killed along the Ohio and Upper Mississippi rivers, where mineral-rich soils enhance antler growth.

The map also illustrates the fantastic hunting and big-buck potential of states like Wisconsin and Illinois, where almost every county produces high numbers of B&C and P&Y bucks.

In addition, the map lists the top 50 counties for record-class buck kills, and shows how many P&Y and B&C bucks each of those counties produced from 1991 to 2000.

To obtain a copy of the poster, contact the QDMA at Box 227, Watkinsville, GA 30677.

Deer Hunting Guide to Full-Moon Dates* in 2003-2004

Month	Date	Day
August	12	Tuesday
September	10	Wednesday
October	10	Friday
November	9	Sunday
December	8	Monday
January	7	Wednesday
February	6	Friday

*Based on Central Standard Time

Plan Your Hunts by the 'Rutting Moon'

In most areas, the rut usually peaks in late October or early November.

Many deer biologists and hunting experts believe it's possible to accurately predict the peak times for deer activity during the rut. Three in-depth research articles on this topic were published in the August, September and October 1997 issues of *Deer & Deer Hunting*. These articles revealed a new theory on the moon's influence on deer activity.

The dates on this page are nearest to the full-moon phases for the rutting months. This guide will help you plan this year's hunts, enabling you to be in the woods when deer are most active.

For an in-depth look at how the moon influences deer behavior, check out Charles Alsheimer's book, *Whitetails by the Moon.*

To order, call (888) 457-2873, or visit our Web site: www.deeranddeerhunting.com.

State Wildlife Agency Contact Info

Alabama Dept. of Wildlife and Freshwater Fisheries
64 N. Union St.
Montgomery, AL 36130
(334) 242-3469 www.dcnr.state.al.us

Arizona Game & Fish Department
2221 W. Greenway Road
Phoenix, AZ 85023
(602) 942-3000 www.gf.state.az.us

Arkansas Game & Fish Commission
#2 Natural Resources Drive
Little Rock, AR 72205
(800) 364-4263 www.agfc.state.ar.us

Colorado Division of Wildlife
6060 Broadway
Denver, CO 80216
(303) 297-1192 www.dnr.state.co.us

Connecticut Dept. of Environmental Protection
391 Route 32
N. Franklin, CT 06254
(860) 424-3105 www.dep.state.ct.us

Delaware Dept. of Natural Resources
89 Kings Hwy., Box 1401
Dover, DE 19903
(302) 739-5295 www.dnrec.state.de.us

Florida Fish & Game Commission
620 S. Meridian Farris Bryant Blvd.
Tallahassee, FL 32399
(850) 488-3641 www.state.fl.us/gfc

Georgia Wildlife Resources
2070 U.S. Hwy. 278 SE
Social Circle, GA 30025
(770) 414-3333 www.dnr.state.ga.us

Idaho Fish & Game Department
Box 25
Boise, ID 83707
(208) 334-3717
www.state.id.us/fishgame/fishgame.html

Illinois Dept. of Conservation
524 S. Second St.
Springfield, IL 62701
(217) 782-7305 www.dnr.state.il.us

Indiana Division of Wildlife
553 E. Miller Drive
Bloomington, IN 47401
(317) 232-4080 www.state.in.us/dnr

Iowa Dept. of Natural Resources
Wallace State Office Bldg.
Des Moines, IA 50319-0034
(515) 281-4687 www.state.ia.us/wildlife/

Kansas Dept. of Wildlife
Box 1525
Emporia, KS 66801
(620) 672-5911 www.kdwp.state.ks.us

Kentucky Dept. of Wildlife
#1 Game Farm Road
Frankfort, KY 40601
(800) 858-1549 www.state.ky.us

Louisiana Dept. of Wildlife
Box 98000
Baton Rouge, LA 70898
(225) 765-2887 www.wlf.state.la.us

Maine Dept. of Inland Fisheries and Wildlife
284 State St., State House Station 41
Augusta, ME 04333
(207) 287-2571 www.state.me.us/ifw

Maryland Division of Wildlife
4220 Steele Neck Road
Vienna, MD 21869
(410) 260-8200 www.dnr.state.md.us

Massachusetts Wildlife
Westborough, MA 01581
(617) 727-1614 www.state.ma.us/dfwele

Michigan Dept. of Natural Resources
Box 30028
Lansing, MI 48909
www.dnr.state.mi.us

Minnesota Dept. of Natural Resources
Box 7, 500 Lafayette Road
St. Paul, MN 55155
(651) 296-4506 www.dnr.state.mn.us

Mississippi Dept. of Conservation
Southport Mall, Box 451
Jackson, MS 39205
(800) 546-4868 www.mdwfp.com

Missouri Dept. of Conservation
Box 180
Jefferson City, MO 65102-0180
(573) 751-4115
www.conservation.state.mo.us

Montana Dept. of Fish and Wildlife
1420 E. Sixth Ave.
Helena, MT 59620
(900) 225-5397 www.fwp.state.mt.us

Nebraska Game and Parks
Box 508
Bassett, NE 68714-0508
(402) 471-0641 www.ngpc.state.ne.us

New Hampshire Fish & Game
Region 1, Rt. 2, Box 241
Lancaster, NH 03584
(603) 271-3422
www.wildlife.state.nh.us

New Jersey Division of Fish & Wildlife
Box 418
Port Republic, NJ 08241
(609) 748-2044 www.state.nj.us/dep/fgw

New York Dept. of Conservation
50 Wolf Road
Albany, NY 12233
(518) 402-8985
www.dec.state.ny.us/website/outdoors

North Carolina Wildlife
512 N. Salisburg St.
Raleigh, NC 27604-1188
(919) 733-3393
www.state.nc.us/wildlife

North Dakota Game Department
100 N. Bismarck Expy.
Bismarck, ND 58501
(701) 328-6300 www.state.nd.us/gnf

Ohio Division of Wildlife
1840 Belcher Drive
Columbus, OH 43224
(614) 265-6300 www.dnr.state.oh.us

Oklahoma Department of Wildlife
1801 N. Lincoln, Box 53465
Oklahoma City, OK 73105
(405) 521-3851 www.state.ok.us

Oregon Dept. of Fish and Wildlife
400 Public Service Bldg.
Salem, OR 97310
(503) 872-5268 www.dfw.state.or.us

Pennsylvania Game Commission
2001 Elmerton Ave.
Harrisburg, PA 17110
(717) 787-4250
www.pgc.state.pa.us

Rhode Island Dept. of Environmental Management
83 Park St.
Providence, RI 02903
(401) 222-6822 www.state.ri.us/dem

South Carolina Dept. of Natural Resources
Box 167
Columbia, SC 29202
(803) 734-3888
www.dnr.state.sc.us

South Dakota Division of Wildlife
Bldg. 445 E. Capital
Pierre, SD 57501
(605) 773-3485
www.state.sd.us/gfp/index.htm

Tennessee Wildlife Resources
Box 407
Nashville, TN 37204
(888) 814-8972
www.state.tn.us/twra

Texas Parks & Wildlife
4200 Smith School Road
Austin, TX 78744
(800) 895-4248 www.tpwd.state.tx.us

Vermont Dept. of Fish and Wildlife
103 S. Main St.
Waterbury, VT 05671
(802) 241-3701 www.anr.state.vt.us

Virginia Dept. of Game and Fisheries
Box 11104
Richmond, VA 23230
(804) 367-1000 www.dgif.state.va.us

Washington Dept. of Fish and Wildlife
600 Capitol Way N.
Olympia, WA 98501
(360) 902-2200 www.wa.gov/wdfw

West Virginia Wildlife Resources
State Capital, Bldg. 3
Charleston, WV 25305
(304) 367-2720 www.wvwildlife.com

Wisconsin Dept. of Natural Resources
101 S. Webster St.
Madison, WI 53707
(608) 266-2621 www.dnr.state.wi.us

Wyoming Game and Fish
5400 Bishop Blvd.
Cheyenne, WY 82002
(900) 884-4263 http://gf.state.wy.us

Leonard Lee Rue III

The Traveling Deer Hunter

Things You Should Know Before Booking a Deer Hunting Trip to Canada

It's no big secret that Canada offers some of the best deer hunting in North America. From British Columbia to Quebec, hunters not only find huge whitetails, they hunt pristine wilderness areas with little from other hunters.

What's more, most Canadian deer hunts are relatively inexpensive, considering many outfitters offer fantastic accommodations and top-notch guide services. However, it's unwise to book any hunt without doing a lot of homework. Although most outfitters offer hunting packages, many details are left to the hunter.

The following items are just a few you should investigate before booking a Canadian hunt. For more information, contact the bureaus and information centers listed within this article.

Tax-Refund Policy

Before writing a check for what seems like an affordable hunt package, double-check to see what taxes you owe. In many cases, package hunts are quoted on price, but they do not include federal and provincial taxes.

Nonresidents are eligible for a reimbursement of 50 percent of the taxes paid on a package. An outfitter who sells a package directly to non-residents can request this reimbursement on their behalf and deduct it from the price of the package.

For more information, contact your outfitter or call Revenue Canada at (613) 991-3346.

Canada's Updated Gun Law

Canada requires visitors to register their firearms. The registration form can be completed in about 10 minutes. However, because it is a declaration, visitors should not sign the form until they are before a customs officer. The fee is $37 ($50 Canadian) per gun.

Trip Cancellation

Whether you are dealing with an outfitter or an intermediary, inquire about cancellation policies. Conditions should appear in the agency's guidelines or the outfitter's brochure.

Agency/Outfitter Responsibility

Canadian hunting agencies serve as intermediaries between travellers and travel service organizations. Because they do not exercise any control over suppliers, agencies cannot be held responsible if the suppliers fail to provide services.

Neither intermediaries nor outfitters can be held responsible for any damage, loss, delay, illness, injury or inconvenience arising from:

✓errors, negligence or omissions on the part of other suppliers, such as carriers, hotels, etc.

✓strikes, mechanical failures, a quarantine or other restrictive government action, meteorological conditions or other factors beyond human control such as forest fires.

✓failure on the part of the customer to carry necessary travel documents.

✓any airport delays on the

CANADA OFFERS some of the best whitetail hunting on the planet. However, your dream hunt could become a nightmare if you don't make the proper preparations before your trip.

customer's day of departure, for whatever reason.

✓material damage, loss of property or theft.

✓illness, injury and/or death.

Insurance

Most agencies offer trip cancellation, medical and baggage insurance. For information on such policies, contact the fishing and hunting agency of your choice.

Terms of Payment

If the trip has not been completely paid for before your departure and you do not intend to settle the bill with cash, you should verify whether the outfitter accepts personal checks, traveler's checks and/or credit cards.

Baggage

Before departure, check if the airline has weight limits and baggage allowances. Most airlines tightly monitor baggage regulations.

Climatic Conditions

While every effort is made to comply with published timetables, irregularities in flight operations can occur in some regions, due to poor weather. Such conditions can also affect the schedule of activities at an outfitter's camp. There is no refund for adjustments to activities resulting from such irregularities.

Permits and Quotas

Hunters must purchase provincial hunting licenses, generally available at sporting goods stores in most cities and towns, and from many outfitters.

Nonresidents are not obliged to produce a hunter's safety certificate to purchase a hunting license.

Deer Hunting

Nonresidents are limited to purchasing particular hunting licenses and frequenting specific hunting zones or areas, according to the species hunted.

Where to Write

Alberta
Department of Forestry,
Lands and Wildlife
Main Floor North Tower
Petroleum Plaza
9045 108th St.
Edmonton, Alberta CAN T5K 2G6

British Columbia
Ministry of Environment,
Fish and Wildlife
780 Blanchard St.
Victoria, British Columbia
CAN V8V 1X5

Manitoba
Dept. of Natural Resources
Wildlife Branch
200 Saulteaux Crescent
Winnipeg, Manitoba,CAN
R3J 3W3

New Brunswick
Bureau of Natural Resources
Fish and Wildlife Branch
Box 6000
Fredricton, N.B. CAN E3B4X5

Newfoundland
Dept. of Culture, Wildlife Division
Box 8750
St. Johns, N.F. CAN A1C 5 7

Nova Scotia
Dept. of Lands and Forests
136 Exhibition St.
Kentville, N.S. CAN B4N 4E5

Ontario
Ministry of Natural Resources
Room 1-73, MacDonald Block
900 Bay St.
Toronto, Ontario CAN M7A 2C3

Quebec
Dept. of Recreation, Hunting
Box 2200, 150 E. St. Cyrille
Quebec City, Quebec, CAN G1R 4Y1

Saskatchewan
Parks and Renewable Resources
3211 Albert St.
Regina, Saskatchewan
CAN S4S 5W6

Nonresidents pursuing whitetails can hunt in all zones where hunting is allowed. However, nonresidents cannot participate in computer drawings to obtain a hunting license for antlerless deer during gun season.

Deer Registration

When returning to the United States from Canada, U.S. hunters must register their kill when going through the U.S. Customs.

Transporting Game

All successful deer hunters must immediately detach the appropriate transportation tag from his or her license and affix it to the deer. The tag must remain affixed throughout the registration process and until the animal has been dressed and stored.

Safety Regulations

All hunters must wear at least 400 square inches of blaze-orange material — covering their back, shoulders and chest — while gun-hunting for deer. The clothing must be visible from all angles at all times.

In addition, a life jacket must be provided for each person using any kind of boat. All boats must be equipped with a bailer, a sound-signaling device and a pair of oars.

Money

It's wise to change your currency into Canadian dollars before leaving the United States. Traveler's checks and major credit cards are accepted in most establishments, but it's advisable to check with your outfitter in advance.

— Daniel E. Schmidt

Miscellaneous Tips and Notes

✓When deer hunting in Manitoba, nonresidents must be accompanied by a licensed Manitoba guide. No more than three hunters can use the services of the same guide at the same time. In addition, nonresident deer hunters must book their hunts through a registered lodge or outfitter.

✓Planning a hunt in Saskatchewan? Topographic maps and aerial photographs can be purchased for all areas of the province from Saskatchewan Environment and Resource Management district offices (except the Regina office). Hunters can also order maps from: Sask Geomatics, 2151 Scarth St., Regina, SK, CANADA S4P 3V7, or call (306) 787-2799.

✓For current weather conditions and extended forecasts in any province, visit Canada's most popular weather Web site: www.weatheroffice.com.

✓Alberta whitetail hunters enjoy tremendous success. Nearly 80,000 hunters pursue whitetails in the province each year, and they harvest about 32,000 deer, a success rate of 40 percent.

Nonresident Fees for Deer Hunting

Province	License*
British Columbia	$75
Alberta	$183
Saskatchewan	$280
Manitoba	$185
Ontario	$123
Quebec	$260

**Nonresident fees as of February 2001. Other fees might apply. For example, Ontario charges a $30 export fee for taking deer out of the province, while Alberta requires hunters to purchase a Wildlife Identification Number for $8. If you plan to hunt deer in Canada, contact the respective province's department of wildlife for complete cost information. Contact information is on Page 199.*

Traveling With Heightened Airport Security

The Sept. 11, 2001, terrorist attacks probably affected air travel forever, especially for those traveling with firearms and ammunition. If you're planning an out-of-state hunt and are depending on air travel to get to your big-buck destination, follow these precautions to ensure your trip goes smoothly.

First, when traveling with a firearm, declare the weapon immediately when you check in at the ticket counter. Also, store the firearm in a locked, airline-approved gun case.

Whenever possible, purchase ammunition when you reach your destination instead of buying it at home and bringing it with you on the plane. However, when flying to remote areas, this might be impossible. In such instances, pack ammunition separately from your firearm in the manufacturer's original package, or locked in a fiber, wood or metal box.

Also, call your airline for information on current policies regarding transporting guns and ammunition. These regulations often change without notice.

When you declare your firearm at the check-in counter, you must show the gun is unloaded and sign a "Firearms Unloaded" declaration.

Keep entry permits in your possession for the country or countries of destination or transit.

Ammunition Restrictions

The amount of ammunition you can check varies by airline. For example, Delta permits passengers to check 11 pounds of ammunition — 10 pounds on its SkyWest flights.

Ammunition weighing more than 11 pounds or containing incendiary projectiles is prohibited.

If necessary, you may purchase a hard-sided, 12-by-52-by-4½-inch gun case with suitcase-type locks for $75 plus tax at most Delta ticket counters.

Airlines generally permit passengers to check one item of shooting equipment as part of their free checked-baggage allowance. One item of shooting equipment is defined as one or a combination of the following:

One firearms case containing:

✓ two or fewer firearms — rifles, pistols or shotguns. Cases containing more than two firearms will be assessed an excess baggage charge.

✓ one shooting mat

✓ one small pistol tool kit

✓ noise suppressors

✓ pistol telescopes

✓ noise suppressors

Finally, remember that each airline might have different firearms restrictions and regulations change, especially in the wake of terrorist activity. Therefore, always call ahead or check your airline's Web site for its latest regulations before packing for your hunting trip.

— National Wild Turkey Federation

Jim Schlender

Myles Keller's Whitetail Tactics: Why Scouting is More Critical Than Hunting

This legendary bow-hunter's off-season plan helps him consistently tag record-class whitetails.

■ *Daniel E. Schmidt*

When he's not traveling the country promoting bow-hunting at sports shows, Myles Keller is in the woods scouting for bow-hunting season. His philosophy? A whitetail hunter can never have too much information about deer behavior and habits.

Being a student of the deer woods helps Keller formulate game plans to outsmart big whitetails with strategic tree-stand placement.

"You always have to be one step ahead, especially if you're trophy hunting," Keller said. "You have to know where the sign is and where deer will move as the season progresses. The days of sitting blindly and killing big deer — well, those days are over."

Keller collects a lot of information by glassing crop fields in summer. This tactic has helped him kill many big bucks in undisturbed, low-traffic areas.

"The bucks are still in bachelor groups at that time," he said. "That allows you to pick out a deer that really inspires you. Yes, they will probably change their habits by hunting season, but in some areas, the early season is a good time to find a buck, pattern him off the fields in the morning and evening and determine some setups. In some states, the season is early enough that you can figure out a way to get close to those big deer."

Here's a look at the simple strategies Keller uses to consistently kill mature bucks. His approach will help you get closer to big deer, but it's critical to err on the side of caution and constantly learn more about your hunting land.

Scout Smart

Scouting new hunting land doesn't need to be exhausting. With some planning and legwork, hunters can quickly assess how deer use the terrain. Hunters should draw their own maps for noting terrain features and deer sign. Major deer runways are easy to find, and they can tell you a lot about deer movements.

For example, a runway that connects different cover types, such as oak forests and pine thickets, likely indicates preferred feeding and bedding areas.

However, don't be fooled into

believing a well-used deer trail is your ticket to a monster buck. Although they use them during the rut, mature bucks seldom travel main runways during daylight early and late in the season.

To outsmart big bucks, use main runways as starting points, and scout the area for parallel trails in fringe cover.

"Serious bow-hunters must do a serious job of scouting and researching the area they will be hunting," Keller said. "You should know the terrain like the back of your hand."

Keller said the post-season is the best time to scout. By then, all foliage is off the trees and other plants, which makes it easy to identify deer trails and sign.

The best way to get a jump on post-season scouting trips is to acquire topographical maps and aerial photos of your hunting land. These tools can reveal terrain features you might be unaware of, and can indicate funnels and travel corridors that connect potential bedding and feeding areas. Keller uses maps and photos to plan hunts around the changing phases of deer season. For example, from prior scouting, Keller might know deer use certain ridges and benches more during the rut than the pre-rut. With his maps and photos, he can devise a game plan for hunting the early season, pre-rut, rut, post-rut and late season.

"Topo maps and aerial photos help you find food sources, fence lines and other connecting areas from bedding areas to feeding areas," he said. "Plan ahead so you can be ready to move your stands during the changing phases.

"Also learn how and when deer use each area. Is it a morning or afternoon route?"

Bed Time

It's difficult — if not impossible — for even consistently successful big-buck hunters like Keller to pinpoint "typical" buck bedding areas. Each situation is different, and it takes hours of pre-season scouting for hunters to unravel big-buck secrets.

Like Keller, Wisconsin's Greg Miller is famous for his no-nonsense approach to scouting. Miller agrees it's difficult to find bedding areas of mature bucks.

"I prefer to search for buck bedding areas during the post-season because of something I call the 'minimal disturbance factor,'" Miller wrote in the March 1999 *Deer & Deer Hunting*. "If there is one time of the year when running a buck out of his bed is less likely to hurt your chances for success, this it it."

Although hunters must be careful not to spread their scent through an area while scouting, they can scout for several hours without worrying about educating mature bucks too much. It might take a few trips, but a hunter cannot begin to understand a big buck's behavior until he knows every inch of its home range.

The Wind Factor

Keller said he doesn't consider hunting a property until he knows every terrain feature. With his mind overloaded with this new information, he carefully determines where he'll place tree stands. Sometimes, Keller cannot use prime areas as stand sites because predominant winds would tip deer to his presence. It's easy to understand why he believes wind direction is the most crucial aspect of stand hunting.

"This is especially important when selecting your routes to stands," he said. "Be prepared to have a stand for all possible wind directions."

For example, imagine your hunting land includes an oak ridge with bedding areas to the east and west. If the predominant wind comes from the southwest, hunt the ridge's northeastern corner. If winds shift, hunt the western corner — if your scent does not blow into the bedding area. The rule for wind? If it's not favorable, do not hunt the stand.

Also, remember that a stand might be positioned correctly for wind direction, but the route to it might not be. Keller said that's why it's important to have more than one route to each stand. The alternative route might require walking twice as far, but the result — an undetected approach — is worth it.

"You're less likely to be patterned," Keller said. "I've killed quite a few bucks with a crosswind approach. This requires you to have a pretty good handle on the directional movement of the deer in your area."

Stand Placement

Finding prime areas to intercept bucks is only part of the equation. Tree-stand placement is critical to success. This is where many hunters fail, according to Keller. He said stand sites must not be tampered with, and stands must be placed with extreme caution.

After selecting a stand site, do not cut large shooting lanes, trim low-hanging branches or make other obvious alterations a buck might notice. If you must clear subtle shooting lanes, do it after the season. Cut saplings and brush as close to the ground as possible, leaving no signs of stumps or fresh cuts. A hunter increases his chances of success by spending as little time as possible at a stand site.

"Keep any pruning to a minimum, and do it early," Keller said. "If you must do some in-season scouting, try to get it done in one day. Numerous scouting trips to one area will kill your chances on a big buck."

Regardless of how careful they are with scent control, hunters invariably leave some scent wherever they walk.

Keller said stands should be hung in trees that provide exceptional background cover. Do not hang stands in mature "telephone pole" trees that offer few branches as a backdrop for breaking up a human outline. Hunters are best served by stands placed above lower-hanging branches.

Don't expect your stand to offer shots in every direction without making a modification or two. Study the site, and erring on the side of camouflage, place the stand so it leaves a couple of shooting options. You might get a second chance at a buck that passes your stand unaware of you. If a second shooting lane isn't available and the buck gets by you, commit him to memory, because it's likely the last time you'll see him. Seldom do you get a second encounter with a mature buck.

Depending on the tree, hang your stand at a height that's comfortable for you. Remember, height isn't as important as camouflage. Scores of hunters consistently kill big bucks from stands at lower heights. It's critical to stay hidden and place stands to take advantage of wind.

Keller said all aspects of tree-stand placement — where, when and how high — should account for hunting pressure. As a rule, he places his stands at least one month before the season. Although he prefers to hunt high — 22 feet is his standard — Keller said heights of about 15 to 20 feet are equally effective at breaking up his outline if there is good background camouflage.

Keller said the direction the sun rises and sets is also important to tree-stand placement, because it can make or break surrounding camouflage. He said hunters should take advantage of the sun's position throughout the day to maximize where they can see and where deer cannot. For example, a morning stand should ideally be placed so the sun is to a hunter's back or side. This lets the hunter see deer approaching and deters deer from looking up.

Public-Land Options

Keller said hunters shouldn't overlook remote tracts of public land when seeking big bucks.

"It's not a kiss of death," he said. "You might have to walk a little farther, but some of these public lands — especially if a guy researches them — are fantastic."

For example, Keller said he recently hunted in Iowa near some public land two men were hunting. The men had scouted the land extensively. Within a couple of days, both tagged 130-class bucks. The key to finding similar success is to find unpressured tracts that hold mature deer.

"When you're dealing with pressured deer, that makes it difficult," Keller said. "I don't like to take my stands down, but in some states you have to. In those instances, I try to have a more portable stand that's quiet."

The same principles hold true when hunting smaller pieces of private land — 30 to 50 acres. Small tracts can produce big bucks, but again, pressure — or lack of pressure — is critical.

"If you have the property to yourself, you can never put up too many stands," Keller said. "The key is to put them up ahead of time without disturbance and be careful not to burn them out by hunting them too much. Having numerous stands allows you to slip in and hunt a stand when the conditions are perfect."

Tree-Stand Hunting Tips

A smart hunting approach is the final key. Although good stand placement and smart wind tactics place hunters in the ballpark, Keller believes many hunters fail because they make careless mistakes.

For example, Keller said he never hunts the same stand more than two consecutive days.

"You should have at least three or four stand sites," he said. "The first couple of times on a stand are probably going to be your best (for seeing a big buck). Use these first times wisely. Only once in a great while will a hunter be able to use his stand for morning and evening hunts."

Hunting season is not the time to investigate areas near your stand.

"Be prepared, and think about what you're doing and why," Keller said. "The stand is not the place to gather information (further scouting). This should already be done."

Buck movement is dependent on the terrain, time of year and hunting pressure in your area, he added.

"Most hunters don't stay in their stands long enough," he said. "You should stay in your stand four or five hours or longer. If you're seeing deer movement — especially during the rut — and you've placed your stand in the right location, almost any time of the day could produce a sighting of a big buck."

Hunters must be ready when the moment of truth arrives. To be prepared, Keller practices shooting his bow at the exact height from which he'll be hunting. A few feet higher or lower can make a difference while hunting. He also shoots from various positions, such as crouching, twisting to each side and turning around the back of his tree stand. To practice these shots, Keller sets up a tree stand in his back yard and tries to position it in the same fashion as stands on his hunting land.

SERIOUS BOW-HUNTERS scout their hunting areas intently. Keller says hunters should know the terrain like the back of their hand.

Conclusion

Keller said the key to hunting record-class bucks is being prepared to accept an unfilled tag.

"In trophy hunting, you're going for something out of the ordinary, and you should be prepared to go home empty-handed," he said.

You can't outsmart mature bucks by halfheartedly scouting and hanging tree stands in spots that look good. Success requires hours of preparation and careful analysis. In the end, knowledge — not just time in a stand — will put you face to face with your dream buck.

Show Us Your Best Buck!

Have you recently tagged your best buck? Send us your notes and photos, and we might publish them in the next edition of *The Little Book of Big Bucks*!

Size does not matter — any buck can be a trophy, especially if it has an interesting story behind it.

Send your contributions to:

Deer & Deer Hunting Magazine
Atn: Big Bucks Book
700 E. State Street
Iola, WI 54990-0001

If we publish your contribution, you will receive a free copy of the book. Sorry, due to the large number of submissions received, photos cannot be returned.